Praise for Tom Slone's *Grounders*

An outstanding work; a captivating and life-changing read. Tom has written a real-world guide to improving our lives in an understandable, riveting, and practical manner. It's a must read, and my business colleagues and children will all receive copies from me. Tom Slone is a true mentor for all of us. I only wish I could have been part of his trip!

—*Michael Gade, former Senior Partner, Coopers & Lybrand; Founding Partner, The Challance Group; Executive in Residence at University of North Texas; Board Member, Rent-a-Center, Inc.*

There's not a person on this planet that can't learn something profound from Tom Slone! Tom embodies mentoring in every aspect of its meaning. He has had a profound impact on my life as a mentor, from his teachings about the fundamentals of successful business practices to his constantly reminding me of how best to encourage, motivate, inspire, and treat others. *Grounders* is a great journey in the fundamentals of life: relationships, children, baseball, and what it means to be a role model. Thank you, Tom, for sharing this journey...

—*T. Charles Pierson, President and CEO, Big Brothers Big Sisters Lone Star*

Grounders is a wonderful story of kids and adults traveling across this great, diverse country and experiencing sports, culture, and friendship....This story is about helping others, learning from life's experiences, and having heroes that care. It is also about a man who learned to help others, always leading by example and caring for his fellow man.

—*Keith Hughes, Former Chairman and CEO, Associates First Capital*

The lessons one can take away from reading *Grounders* are important ones. They are applicable to a number of venues and can be of great assistance in keeping an individual "well-grounded"....Congratulations on a book that is an enjoyable read and a reminder of some very important lessons to enhance any journey.

—*Nan Dearen Gluntz, former Director, Big Brothers Big Sisters of Fort Worth*

In *Grounders*, Tom Slone demonstrates that he's an all-star mentor, businessman, teacher, fundraiser, and storyteller. Sit down with this book and a bag of peanuts, and watch him hit a home run.

—*Joseph M. McQuillan, Chairman of QTI Service Corporation, Treasurer of Las Colinas Parks Foundation, and former Vice Chairman of Associates First Capital*

I found *Grounders* to be an enjoyable read that showcases Tom Slone's passion for developing and leading people. The mentoring and leadership tools Tom has developed over a long and successful career in both business and philanthropy are artfully woven into his narrative account of a 20-day dream roadshow he led with seven young men in tow. This roadshow provided many opportunities to teach important life lessons and an enjoyable account of the trials and tribulations you might expect from being on the road with seven young men. This is a book you may choose to read every year to truly benefit from its message.

—*Roy A. Guthrie, former Executive Vice President and Chief Financial Officer, Discover Financial Services*

Grounders is an insightful book that contains life and business lessons that will make you stop and take stock of how you do both....So get your glove and unleash your heart and mind, and go with us on an incredible life journey.

—*Gary Randle, founder and Executive Director of H.O.P.E. Farm*

Tom Slone epitomizes the American Dream. I cherish his friendship, and am honored that I am part of *Grounders*. Tom has the charisma, intelligence, determination, and empathy required to be a great mentor....I recall when he took a group of youngsters to Florida to meet the Marlins baseball team, to sit in the owners' seats as special guests of the team, to meet the players, and to watch a game....I know those kids will remember the trip and Tom—and that, like him, they will strive to become mentors to those coming up behind them.

—*Norman Rales, former owner of the Texas Rangers,*
philanthropist, and President of Kenwood Financial

I read *Grounders*...and started to wish that you would go to ten more ballparks. It is a neat piece of history in the making. The description of the characters made me feel as if I knew them by the end of the trip...and your words of wisdom and advice will make for memories over a lifetime. Thank you for letting me get my nose under the tent!

—*Vince J. Kiernan II, President Emeritus and Managing Director*
of International Milbar/Stride Corporation

Great life lessons throughout. As I read it, I resonated with the discipline and common sense you deploy in your own life....I very much enjoyed it and smiled when I read about your mentors because you're one of mine.

—*Ron Nicol, Global Leader of the Technology, Media, and Telecommunications Practice, The Boston Consulting Group*

If you are a fan of baseball, you will love *Grounders*. This is a once-in-a-lifetime true story in which the author and two friends take a group of young boys (Tom's three grandsons and two of their friends and two boys from H.O.P.E. Farm) to ten games in ten cities in twenty-one days. *Grounders* is an exhilarating and well-written book on mentoring and a lesson for all of us to learn. You will be moved by this book.

—*Christa Overcash, widow of Reece Overcash, former Chairman and Chief Executive Officer of Associates First Capital*

Grounders

A Once-in-a-Lifetime Journey of Baseball, History, and Mentoring

Tom Slone

Introduction by Tony Jeary

Photo by Fred Piggee

Touchstone Communications
545 Nolen Drive, Suite 300
Southlake, Texas 76092
touchstonebpo.com

For permission to reprint all or part of this book, to order copies in bulk, or to arrange a talk or presentation by Tom Slone, contact Glenda Garrett at Touchstone Communications, 545 Nolen Drive, Suite 300, Southlake, TX 76092, phone: 817-500-5007; fax: 972-852-1834; ggarrett@ touchstonebpo.com.

For my wife Frances,
for letting us go on this grand journey without her

Table of Contents

The Opening Pitch:
Guidance from a World-Class Coach
by Tony Jeary

We are successful when we achieve the objectives we have established in advance. Anything else is chance or serendipity.

The most successful people live their lives on purpose. They don't sit around waiting to see what might happen next. They know what they want, and they are clear and focused about how they will achieve it.

This is true in baseball, in business, in mentoring, and in life.

Tom Slone understands success. He also understands baseball, business, and the art of mentoring. Tom's multiple areas of expertise, and his willingness to share what he has learned, make *Grounders* a compelling and important book.

But Tom offers us much more. He also knows how to deliver a pithy lesson and make it stick—in part by focusing on the essentials, in part by telling a good story.

Tom Slone

In *Grounders*, Tom combines the inspiring and entertaining story of a grand baseball journey with 33 essential lessons that all of us (yes, even those of us who are already very successful) can apply in our lives. He also demonstrates, over and over, the life-changing power of mentoring.

But don't take my word for it. Turn the page, pay attention as Tom steps up to the plate, and watch him hit a home run.

Tony Jeary is a strategic facilitator, a success accelerator, a master presenter, and a coach to top CEOs around the world. His many books include Strategic Acceleration, Speaking from the Top, Persuade Any Audience, The Secrets of Meeting Magic *(with George Lowe), and* Finding 100 Extra Minutes a Day. *You can learn more about Tony at tonyjeary.com.*

Chapter 1
Warmup

On October 27, 2010, my wife Frances and I stood in the infield at Rangers Ballpark in Arlington, looking up at a crowd 43,000 people. The first game of the World Series was about to begin.

Along with 78 other season ticket holders, we had just unfurled a huge American flag, which we held tightly but carefully as the fans sang our national anthem. I was proud to represent America's veterans, but I was also proud of my home team, the Texas Rangers, which had made it to the World Series for the first time after almost 50 years of trying.

Until 2010, the Rangers had a less-than-stellar record. In fact, as Wikipedia put it, "The Rangers franchise and their fans had a long history of futility and disappointment."

Back in the fall of 2004, after the Texas Rangers failed to make the playoffs for the umpteenth time—and I felt bitterly disappointed for the umpteenth time—I decided that I needed a reason other than a winning season to renew my enthusiasm for baseball. I began thinking about taking a trip to see Major League Baseball played in several different cities, and I envisioned taking my three grandsons, Matt, Sam, and Andy, with me.

Tom and Frances Slone with the giant flag they helped to unfurl at Rangers Ballpark in Arlington, Texas at the beginning of the 2010 World Series.

By the time we actually left, ten months later, the trip had morphed into a major expedition. We saw 10 games in 10 cities over a period of 21 days. I was accompanied by two of my close friends, Gary Randle and Mike Meyer, as well as by my three grandsons, some of their friends, and two boys from an after-school program, H.O.P.E. Farm, which Gary runs. During the last seven games, Mike's father, Bob, took

Mike's place, and during our visit to Cincinnati, a small army of relatives and friends joined us for a day at the new Great American Ball Park, which is right on the Ohio River.

We began our trip with a flight to Miami to see the world-champion Marlins play our own Texas Rangers. In the three weeks that followed, we also visited Atlanta, Washington, DC, Cincinnati, Pittsburgh, Philadelphia, New York, Boston, Milwaukee, and Chicago. The plan was to stay two to three days in the larger cities and less time in others. Ultimately, we spent an extra day in DC, almost three days in New York, and two days in Philadelphia, Boston, Chicago, and Milwaukee (where we also visited the Harley-Davidson factory). In every city, our travels provided the boys with opportunities to learn important lessons about life, baseball, and our wonderful country—and equally valuable opportunities for me and a few other adults to teach those lessons. We grown-ups learned a few things along the way, too.

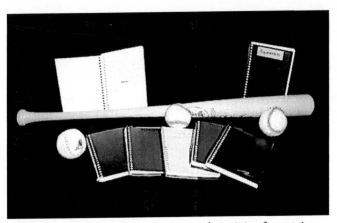

Photographer Fred Piggee captures the spirit of our trip.

After the trip ended, many people encouraged me to write a book chronicling the experiences we had, the things we learned, and, most importantly, how we adults used the trip to mentor these young boys of different ages, races, and backgrounds.

Since that time, several people I admire and trust have encouraged me to expand the book to demonstrate the value and power of mentoring. They also suggested that I include not only the lessons the boys learned on our trip, but many of the most important lessons I've learned and taught as a mentor, fundraiser, Fortune 500 business executive, and entrepreneur over the past 40 years. You're holding the results in your hands.

As you'll discover, mentoring, growing up, running a business (whether in the U.S. or in a third-world country), and playing baseball—or any sport—have many similarities, and many important things to teach us. Enjoy.

Lesson 1
Helping One Boy at a Time

My friend Gary Randle runs H.O.P.E. Farm, an after-school program for African-American boys in one of the most crime-filled neighborhoods of Fort Worth. (H.O.P.E. stands for Helping Other People Excel.) Each day at H.O.P.E.

Farm, Gary Randle provides one-on-one mentoring to each of his 40+ mentees. The five or six minutes these boys each receive daily from Gary are often the best—and sometimes the only—personal attention they receive from adults all day.

Every day each boy meets with Gary to review what he did that day at home and at school. If he has done well, he gets a knuckle bump, praise, and a bear hug. These rewards never get old; the boys' faces light up like Christmas trees every time. They are anxious to see the happiness in Gary's face and to experience his loving words of congratulations.

If a boy has not done well, Gary tells him in a stern voice to take a seat. The boy then has to watch and wait as the other boys collect their rewards. After the other boys have gotten their knuckle bumps and bear hugs, Gary asks the boy to explain exactly what he did wrong, what he will do to correct the situation, and what he will do differently next time. Most of the boys don't have two bad days in a row. And even when a boy does have a bad day, he still has high self-esteem. He'll look Gary in the eye and explain earnestly what he did wrong and how he will correct it.

This one-on-one mentoring is used with great success at H.O.P.E. Farm. Whether Gary is giving out praise, instruction, inspiration, or correction, every boy gets this daily face time—and every boy hungers for it. For many it is the high point of their day.

We see the same approach at every baseball practice, from Little League through the Major Leagues. In fact, in all my years of playing sports, whether it was baseball or basketball, I never had a coach tell us what to do and then leave.

The coach always gave immediate direction to individuals—perhaps not with the loving tone that Gary uses, but in an effective manner nevertheless.

Kids and adults who have played sports relish this one-on-one training. I once overheard one of my direct reports tell another, "If Tom Slone stops giving you individual attention and instructions, you'll know he's given up on you." The other's response was, "Boy, he must really think I have a lot of potential, then!"

We need to give more of this one-on-one direction, especially in the business world.

Too many leaders and managers use criticism instead of correction, direction, and instruction. They take out their frustrations on people they know nothing about. Or they treat each performance review as a mere task to complete, when they could instead use it to learn about the person, listen to their goals, understand their challenges, and help them grow.

About 18 months after creating a company in Pakistan, my co-owner and I introduced quarterly performance reviews for all employees. This was completely foreign to them. To my surprise, these reviews were received with a great deal of enthusiasm, many smiles, and a feeling of purpose. Taking the time to sit down with each person, one on one, proved to be one of the most powerful forms of motivation we could have provided. The results have been astonishing: in a workforce of over 300 people, our employees have a 95% average attendance rate each day, and we have had an annual turnover of only 5% in the eight years we have been in existence.

This is in a field that typically experiences 100% turnover *each year*.

One-to-one mentoring is a win-win-win-win: a win for the person being mentored; a win for the person doing the mentoring; a win for the community where the mentee and mentor live; and a win for the organization where they work.

Mentoring helps people find and keep jobs, make money, and succeed. It helps them do good work for their employers, so that *they* can succeed. It keeps people—especially young males—out of prison. And it saves tons and tons of money. It costs about $45,000-$50,000 a year to keep someone in prison. It costs less than $1,000 a year to mentor a child through Big Brothers Big Sisters. You do the math and decide what makes the most sense.

Lesson 2
Pay Attention to Your Plan

When you create any kind of a plan, you need to understand where you are going, what you hope to accomplish, how you are going to get there, and who will go with you on the journey. This is true whether you're planning a baseball trip with a group of young men, starting a business, raising money for a university or a nonprofit, or building a career.

Creating any detailed plan—whether it's a plan to build a new business, grow a non-profit organization, or take a group of boys to baseball games all around the country— also requires a deep knowledge of who is going to be affected by it, and how. This means asking yourself some probing questions. For example: *What will the kids want to get out of the trip? What return on investment will funders want? Who will donate money for this cause, and how much will each donor likely contribute?*

Whether there are ten, a hundred, or a thousand stakeholders, the secret is to become very clear about how your plan gets you to your goal. This is accomplished through:

- Research

- Experience

- Asking questions

- Communicating clear, consistent messages to stakeholders

- Building appropriate rewards (both external and internal) into the plan

Pay special attention to who will go with you on the journey. Don't be afraid of getting other people involved— but make sure you get the right people. Everyone who helps you create your plan should have the same goals you do— and should agree that the plan will get you there.

Chapter 2
Life's Lessons Begin Early

O n most days, I feel that I'm the luckiest person in the world, because throughout my life I've had many people who cared for me, encouraged me, and mentored me. I didn't always realize it at the time, but I am who I am because of them. Several of them will be mentioned in these pages.

Being a mentor, or learning from a mentor, can take many different forms—and with kids, mentoring is often an everyday, every minute thing. Young people watch what you do and don't do, and listen to what you say (and don't say)— and they learn from all of it.

In the 50s and 60s, when I was growing up, the word "mentor" was not widely used. Although I had many mentors, I knew these people as teachers, coaches, ministers, family members, and heroes of adventure shows on black-and-white TV.

Our grandparents raised my brother and me, since our dad was in the military in Europe, and our mother was in jail for kiting checks. The first person who deeply influenced my life—my first strong and consistent mentor—was my grandfather. Among many other things, he taught me the value of telling the truth when I was just six years old.

I remember the key incident well. I told my grandmother a lie, and she immediately recognized it as such. To teach me a lesson, she announced that she was going to wash out my mouth with soap. In order to avoid that punishment, I told her lie #2—I insisted that I had never told lie #1, and claimed that she must have misunderstood me. That only made her madder. She said, "You never have to remember what you've said if you always tell the truth."

Then my grandfather intervened. He said, "If Tommy said he didn't say it, I believe him." My grandmother threw her hands in the air and stalked off. Then I looked at my grandfather. He was looking hard at me. We both knew what I had done. I had avoided the punishment of the soap, but now I felt crushed by guilt. The valuable lesson I learned that day has stuck with me for over 63 years.

On that day I learned that if you disappoint a person who trusts you, the guilt you'll feel will be far more painful than any lumps you might have to take for saying sincerely, "I screwed up and I'm sorry." Saying that one simple sentence also makes you a better person.

My next mentor was my third grade teacher, Mrs.

Murphy, a white-haired, no-nonsense lady who kept a tight rein on her students. She was the first person who ever used positive reinforcement on me in the classroom. I was the class clown, and on multiple occasions she told me, "You have the ability to laugh at yourself, and to make other people laugh, too. Your personality will always be a huge asset for you, so use it to your advantage." From the third grade on, I've followed her advice, and most of the time it has paid off for me. (As an adult, I've also learned that laughter opens doors in just about every culture.) I've found that even in third-world countries such as Pakistan, where I've run a company for eight years, laughter is universal. In fact, as my wife Frances says, "It's a good place to use your old material."

Once my father returned from overseas, he became my most important mentor. He believed in giving constructive criticism, which at the time I didn't take as very constructive; in not asking for favors; and in contributing an honest day's work for an honest day's pay. He felt a job well done was its own motivation and its own reward. He taught me the importance of discipline, of respect (including self-respect), and of doing things right the first time. He often said—and this became one of the lessons in this book—"If you have to choose between someone liking you or respecting you, go for the respect." I certainly respected my father—and, as I got older, I grew to like him as well.

The night before he died, he said, "Tommy, I wish I had given you boys more." He was thinking of material things, but as our mentor, he gave us more than he realized—things that have gotten my brother Don and me successfully through life.

I had many other mentors in my life, many of them teachers and coaches. But the next ones I want to highlight here were four of my superiors at Associates First Capital. When I worked at Associates in the 70s, 80s, and 90s, it was the 42nd largest company in the United States. For over 30 years, Associates had several exceptional leaders at the top, including Chairman and Chief Executive Officer Reece Overcash, Chairman Keith Hughes, and Vice Chairman Joe McQuillan. But the most inspiring leader, and the one who mentored me the most, was Walt Wileman, whom I reported to for several years. Walt taught me a wide range of operational skills. He was the first master psychologist I ever experienced. He knew how to wisely use both discipline and positive reinforcement. Walt used humor often, as well, and he taught me the importance of reading about other great people and new ideas. He challenged me to think outside the box, to set goals and expectations high, and to provide close follow-up (this was the key). He also taught me how to speak and dress for success.

One day, after a meeting, Walt called me into his office, shut the door, closed the curtains on the window, and said, "Tom, one of these days you're going to be in front of a lot of people, so you need to learn how to tie your tie properly. You don't want to have that big knot under your chin." He had me take off my tie, and he showed me how to tie it in a way that would impress people.

If you think that sounds silly, think again. Ten years later, while getting my shoes shined in Bristol, Tennessee, a young man asked me how I got that little crease in my tie. So I did what Walt had done for me—I showed him how it was done.

Some 40 years after that, while attending the grand opening of a new company in Dallas, I ran into Dion Sanders, the Hall of Fame wide receiver for the Dallas Cowboys, who was attending as a guest celebrity. Dion looked at my tie and said, "Come over here and get your picture taken with me—and show me how you tied that tie." Afterward, I called Walt and suggested that he start his own consulting business in tie tying.

The leaders of Associates also stressed giving back to the community and to the world. We were encouraged to share some of our money, time, and talent with the United Way, Meals on Wheels, Adopt-a-School, the Salvation Army, and many other wonderful causes. My wife and I soon got deeply involved in Big Brothers Big Sisters (BBBS) and Adopt-a-School. Our own kids were already grown, so this gave me a second chance to help mold young lives.

At Big Brothers Big Sisters of Fort Worth, I met a few fantastic mentors, especially Nan Dearen Gluntz, then the director, and Richard Minker, a longtime board member. Nan and Richard were master psychologists who helped me use many of the things I had learned in business to mentor young kids. BBBS soon became a passion for me, and eventually I became chairman of BBBS Fort Worth's board, a position I held for several years. During these years we were able to consolidate the three area Big Brothers Big Sisters agencies into one. Today, in terms of matching contributions and financial strength, it is the largest BBBS agency in the world.

After 32 years at Associates—and 32 years of working long hours, six days a week—I decided to retire. Running an operation with $33 billion in assets and 14,000 employees had taken its toll on me. Yet, although I had planned and executed many things over those 32 years, I hadn't put much thought into what I would do when I didn't have to go to work every day. My thought was to volunteer full time and run the Big Brothers Big Sisters operation in Fort Worth.

When I told this to my boss, Chairman Keith Hughes, he said, "Tom, instead of retiring, why don't you stay around for another year—but we'll change your title and job description. You can be the national Associates Volunteer Executive of Big Brothers Big Sisters. You'll keep your salary, your company car, your office, and your administrative assistant." You've already figured out that I jumped at this opportunity.

A few years earlier I had met Gary Randle, who has taken mentoring to another level at H.O.P.E. Farm. (I introduced you to Gary and H.O.P.E. in the previous chapter.) In its after-school program, African American boys receive mentoring from caring adults, meet and learn from positive role models, and experience consistent respect, concern, and love. Gary and I quickly became good friends, but Gary has also been a mentor for me.

None of us learns to build a life on our own. It's because of our mentors—our wisest teachers, coaches, parents, grandparents, bosses, and other role models—that we are able do what we do. Everyone can benefit from good mentors—

and every young person needs them. Some older ones do, too.

Almost any caring adult can be a good mentor. We have the makings of millions of mentors in our country today. We'd have many, many more than we do now if people only realized how easy mentoring can be.

You already know that I used to be a class clown. So here's a closing joke that my father—my most important mentor—told me about how people come to be who they are.

Two young men begin talking at a party. "What's your name?" one of them asks the other.

"7."

"That's a strange name. Where did you get a name like that?"

"My dad pulled it out of a hat."

"Doesn't that make you mad, having a number as a name?"

"Oh, no. I'm just glad it's not 7¼."

Every time I tell that story, I remember my dad's smile.

Lesson 3
Choose Respect Over Being Liked

My father drummed into my head a very important lesson: if you have a choice between being respected versus being liked, take respect every time. He said, "If you make the right choices, people's respect for you will last forever—but being liked can change in a second."

Over time, I learned that this is because respect is the natural result of integrity and consistency—things each of us has control over. Being liked, however, is mostly the result of fads, luck, and other people's moods—none of which we can control.

Lesson 4
Mentors Are Not Always Friends

Mentors show up in many different forms and situations. Some are relatives, friends, teachers, or coaches you'll stay in touch with throughout your life. Others you'll never see again—but you may remember what they taught you for a lifetime.

Some mentors are sought out; some will seek you out; some will show up through what appears to be happenstance. Some may even come disguised as foes, competitors, or critics—but they may teach you something very valuable nevertheless.

You never know how, where, or when a mentor may appear—or what form their mentoring may take.

Chapter 3
The Value of H.O.P.E.

H.O.P.E. Farm is a Christian-based program for boys between the ages of 5 and 18. The facility is located in the middle of a high-crime area where boys' role models are most likely to be pimps and drug dealers. Dozens of African American boys come daily after school, where they are tutored by top-notch teachers dedicated to giving them an equal chance with kids in more affluent areas of Fort Worth.

All the boys at H.O.P.E. Farm have several things in common. They are being raised without fathers—by single mothers, aunts, and grandmothers. To get admitted to the H.O.P.E. Farm program, a boy's guardian must pay $10 per semester, and must commit to being involved with the boy's behavior and study habits at school and at home. They also must agree that no adult male will live in their home.

I met H.O.P.E. Farm's co-founder and director, Gary Randle, through a mutual acquaintance in 2000. I had become chairman of the board of Big Brothers Big Sisters of Fort Worth and the full-time director of the Tarrant County BBBS office. (This was immediately after my year as the Executive BBBS National Volunteer at Associates.) When I first took on these roles, about 65% of our Littles (in Big Brothers Big Sisters, the mentoring adults are called Bigs and our mentees are called Littles) were African American—yet we didn't have any black employees, or any black representation on our board. This made no sense to me, so I asked Gary to help me change things. He introduced me to many smart, caring people of color who shared our organization's vision, and over the next twelve months the board and staff of BBBS became more representative of the people we serve.

Gary Randle is tall (6' 9"), with personality plus. My friend Bob Meyer, who made the baseball trip with us, said of Gary, "He makes Will Rogers sound like an introvert." Gary was a star basketball player at Texas Christian University, where he also excelled in the classroom. After graduation, he stayed in Fort Worth and became a policeman with the Juvenile Division, where he worked for 15 years. As a cop, Gary saw firsthand what happens to young men when they have the wrong mentors in their lives.

In 1980, Gary and Noble Crawford founded H.O.P.E. Farm to help boys become socially, spiritually, and financially healthy, so that they can be positive forces in their community. Gary and Noble bought several abandoned homes and converted them into a modern and attractive facility. Every weekday, boys come here after school to study and receive guidance from caring adults. Then they are served a hot dinner on china, which they eat with real (not plastic) silverware. After dinner they clean up the tables, vacuum the floor, and get help with their homework.

Some of the kids at H.O.P.E. Farm have backgrounds so tragic that it's a wonder they can hold a conversation. Yet most do well in school. All of them treat one another with respect, and they are both confident and polite.

One young man I met had been kept locked in a closet, with nothing to eat, by his mother and her boyfriend. After several weeks, he began to eat the carpet. He was found almost dead and taken to the hospital. When he recovered enough to go home, he was taken in by an aunt and enrolled in the H.O.P.E. Farm program. At first he continually hoarded food—even catsup. But today he is healthy and good-natured, with no eating disorders—and his grades are excellent. His mother and her boyfriend are still in prison.

Most of the boys at H.O.P.E. Farm get A's and B's in school and high scores on national tests. Many go on to college.

My friendship with Gary and his family has grown steadily over the years. So has my connection with H.O.P.E. Farm and its staff.

When I first told Gary about the baseball trip I planned to take with my grandsons, he said, "Tom, that sounds like every boy's dream trip. In fact, I wish *I* could go on a trip like that." (Later, when I told other people about the trip, almost every adult male had the same reaction.)

I soon realized that I wanted Gary to come along, too—partly to help supervise the boys, and partly so I could have a friend of my own with whom I could share the experience. (My wife is not a big baseball fan.)

But I knew that I needed to take the planning one step at a time. First I needed to get my grandsons on board.

Lesson 5
Plan B Sometimes Outperforms Plan A

In both business and life, having a backup plan is crucial for anything worth doing. We choose Plan A because we believe it will yield the best results—but often, when Plan A becomes impossible, Plan B may create far better results than we ever imagined.

Gary Randle created H.O.P.E. Farm because his original mentoring plan—his Plan A—failed. When he was a Fort Worth policeman, he was the mentor of a troubled 12-year-old boy whose father was in prison. After only a few months of Gary's mentoring at the beginning of the school year, the boy's attitude changed, and his attendance and grades improved dramatically. The young man's teachers were amazed at his progress.

Then, over the Christmas break, the young man went to see his father in prison. As a result of that one encounter, he reverted back to all his old habits. He shed everything Gary taught him like a snake getting rid of its skin. Gary had gotten to him too late.

However, that failure led Gary to develop a Plan B. Today he mentors dozens of boys from the ages of 5 to 18 after school. He has done this for over 20 years at H.O.P.E. Farm, and it works consistently.

The lesson here: Don't get too upset when Plan A doesn't work out. Have a Plan B ready, and don't be afraid to go to it!

Lesson 6
Forgiveness

Although H.O.P.E. Farm provides quick and clear consequences for every mistake or infraction, it also provides forgiveness. When a boy makes a mistake or disappoints someone, Gary has the boy acknowledge it. Then the two discuss the reason for the poor choice, and Gary and the young man correct it.

This works because Gary also provides quick and continuous follow-up, clear and appropriate communication, and the right rewards.

This is an ideal formula for mentoring of all types.

Lesson 7
Stop, Look, and Listen

At H.O.P.E. Farm, each person is responsible for their actions and choices—and for the results of those actions and choices. Furthermore, when you make the right choices, you start to feel good about yourself. Your self-esteem grows.

These don't have to be profound choices. They can be as simple as choosing how you present yourself to others. During my first visit to H.O.P.E. Farm, Gary instructed each boy to "take care of business," which meant introducing themselves to me. The boys stood in a line and greeted me one at a time. Each young man came up to me, looked me straight in the eye, and said, "My name is _____. I'm very pleased to meet you."

I asked Gary how long it took these young men to be able to do this. Gary responded, "Two to three weeks."

These young men presented themselves with far more confidence and poise than most young people I've met from families with many advantages.

After meeting these boys, I began to pay more attention to the simple act of looking people in the eye. To my surprise, I found that very few kids routinely practice it. What is more disconcerting is that few adults do it during interviews, meetings, and performance reviews. Yet there is a very high correlation between high self-esteem, high productivity, and being able to look your boss in the eye.

The boys at H.O.P.E. Farm know something that many adults don't.

Lesson 8
Second Chances

In today's world, not everyone gets a second chance. Kids who grow up in dangerous homes and neighborhoods often don't. One mistake, or one moment of thoughtlessness, can mean a beating—or, out on the street, a violent death.

Each year our company sponsors a Christmas party for the boys of H.O.P.E. Farm. The boys are each given a gift that they have specifically asked for.

Last Christmas, Gary told two of the boys that they couldn't open their gifts. When my wife asked him why, he explained, "Those two boys misbehaved at school, and I received notes from their teachers. They need to learn that if they mess up even once, it can have huge consequences. I don't give them second chances because the circumstances of their lives don't give them second chances. I don't want to see any of these boys shot dead because he thought he'd get do-overs."

It's a powerful lesson—and the boys got it.

Chapter 4
The Players and the Game Plan

I originally envisioned a trip that would last all summer, and that would take us to all the Major League Baseball parks in the United States. I quickly realized that this wouldn't be possible. For one thing, I had recently started a new company in Pakistan, and I couldn't be away from it for an entire summer. For another, my teenage grandsons had commitments of their own (sports teams, girlfriends, etc.). So I decided that we would see as many of the Major League stadiums east of the Mississippi that we could in 21 days. I especially wanted to visit Yankee Stadium, Fenway Park, and Wrigley Field, because much of the history of baseball took place in these parks.

When I began planning the trip, my oldest grandson, Matt, was 15. He lived in Pittsburgh, where he had a girlfriend and an active life. He played basketball, wrestled, and had made the Little League baseball all-star team several times. Like many teenage boys, though, he often acted aloof and distanced himself from adults, including me.

Andy, my second oldest grandson, lived in southern Indiana. He, too, was reserved around me. I suspected that his mom—my daughter—had told him I was a perfectionist. (I admit that sometimes I am.) I also knew that she had told him not to act like a kid, which is a hard thing for a kid to do. Andy was generally shy around adults and had trouble looking them in the eye when he talked to them, which wasn't very often. Andy had things to be proud of, though: he had a high IQ, played in his high school band, and was on the football team.

Sam, Matt's younger brother, was 12. In many ways he was the opposite of both his brother and his cousin. He loved people, was always poking fun at his big brother (and often physically poked him in the arm and side as well), and had many friends. He was small for his age, but that didn't stop him from playing football and baseball. In fact, he was quite an athlete. He tore his ACL at the age of 10 playing football, laid out a year, and was now back on the field as a linebacker and receiver. He had a ready smile and an "I want to be around you" personality.

I knew that all three boys enjoyed watching live baseball. But would they want to make the trip with their grandfather? They all seemed very busy, and Matt and Andy weren't comfortable around most adults, including me. Also, my idea of a good time was to go to some ball games, eat, and go home before 9:30 p.m. I knew that might not resonate with them.

I ran the idea by my wife. Her first question was, "What about our four granddaughters? They'll expect you to do the same for them." I said, "They don't like baseball. What if you were to take a trip with them sometime soon, to a place *they'd* like to visit?" "Maybe," Frances said.

Then I ran the idea by the boys' parents, who both said the same thing: "If you can get these wild things out of our house for a month—or, better yet, all summer—we're all for it. This will give us some time to air out their rooms. In fact, we'll help you sell the idea to our kids." I had made it to first base.

Next I wrote each of the boys a letter, telling them about the trip (which at that point was almost a year away). I shamelessly bribed them. I told each one that if he earned all A's and B's, he could go on the trip and take along a friend. I also told each one that if he did want to go, he needed to write me a letter telling me why, and to give me the name of the friend he wanted to take.

I received a letter back from each of the boys very quickly. All were quite excited about going. Sam and Andy took along friends; Matt decided to go solo.

At this point I asked Gary Randle if I could also take two boys from H.O.P.E. Farm. I would hold them to the same standards I set for my grandsons: they had to get all A's and B's in school for a year, and each had to write me a letter saying why he wanted to go. Gary's response was, "Sure, you can take two of my boys—if I can come, too." I was thrilled, since I'd wanted Gary's company all along. I'd made it to second.

It was critical for Gary to go with us, because without him, the guardians of the boys from H.O.P.E. Farm wouldn't let the boys join us. They knew and trusted Gary, but they didn't know me, and at first they were understandably suspicious about why I would want to take their boys on an all-expense-paid trip for three weeks.

The boys from H.O.P.E. Farm were Kamerron and Cameron. Their names were pronounced the same, which occasionally created some confusion. Kamerron was 13; Cameron was 12. They were excited to join us, and I was excited to have them.

Cameron had been raised by his mom; his dad was completely absent from his life. He was a good athlete who played football. He was also the most enthusiastic photographer of the group. He took several hundred photos and videoed everything, from people to stadiums to food. As I discovered later, it was the possibility of going on the baseball trip that turned Cameron around at school. Here's what he wrote in his journal on the first day of our journey:

> *It was hard work getting here. We had to have good grades and great behavior every day.*

Kamerron had an infectious smile on his face all the time. He had been raised by his grandmother and did not know either of his parents. He made friends quickly, was eager to see and explore everything, and loved to eat. Before our trip he had never been on an airplane before, and his comments as a first-time flyer were:

I really enjoyed being above the clouds and going through them.

Here's what he said about the trip:

At first I was failing three classes. I said to myself, "Do you want to go on this trip or not?" So, I started turning in all my daily work and doing well on tests. I thought I would have to go to summer school, but then my teacher told me I would not have to go. I said, "Thank you, God." Now I'm on this trip just as I dreamed to do.

Some of the journals the young men—and the adults—kept every day.

Then there were my grandsons' friends. Jimmy, Sam's friend, was a real pleasure to be around. He was friendly and upbeat—a people-pleaser. He showed up the first day wearing a University of Kentucky t-shirt. I knew at once that this was deliberate, and that he had asked around to learn the name of my favorite college team. He has the skills to get elected to high public office some day. Spencer, Andy's buddy, was something of a smart aleck, often challenging the rules and pushing the envelope. He was never mean-spirited or obnoxious, but he had a way of getting into minor incidents.

When I first began thinking about the trip, I also considered including Mike Meyer, my business partner and close friend. But someone needed to run our business for most of those three weeks that we'd be gone. So we compromised. Mike and his son Jake joined us for the first few days. Then Mike and Jake headed back home, and Mike's dad, Bob, who loves baseball more than anyone I know, became part of our gang for the last 17 days. Bob loves kids, apple pie, and baseball. The journal he kept during our trip captured the sounds and smells of the stadiums we visited, the trains and planes that got us around, and the spirits of the boys. Here are some of his observations:

> *Cameron has unlimited potential; he just needs guidance. He is eager to learn, polite, and lovable.*
>
> *Kamerron is a very lovable young man; needs to be hungry for education; more discipline in his eating habits. Gary makes a huge difference in his life.*

Sam will do well in life; resilient, enthusiastic. He strives to please.

Matt is a mystery to me. Stays within himself; more private.

Andy is a work in progress; acts out sometimes to attract attention; has a big heart.

Spencer is lovable, enthusiastic, daring, and fun-loving. He has an ornery side. Will need strong parenting.

We were a strange lot. Gary is very tall but has poor eyesight. He always walked in the back of the group, so that he could see the people in front of him. (But he often couldn't tell who was missing.) Bob has great eyesight but a hearing problem, so he complemented Gary nicely. We traveled well together everywhere except at subway turnstiles. Bob couldn't hear if his token had dropped, and Gary couldn't see how to put his token in the slot. By working together we never missed a train.

I usually walk fast, so I was often in front of the pack. So there would be me up front; a tall, white-haired gentleman behind me; a very tall African American man bringing up the rear; and a bunch of lost-looking boys between us. To strangers, they must have looked like they were being herded—which sometimes they were.

I've been asked many times why I made the trip. Here is what I tell people. First, I wanted my grandsons, and several other young people, to have the trip of a lifetime. I also wanted them to experience something that I didn't take the time to do with my own kids, but now wished I had. When our kids were growing up, I focused heavily on my career and my education, and spent less time than I should have with them. My kids often wanted to hang out with me, but much of the time I was too busy with something else. Although I have a great relationship with my kids, I regret not being around for them more often when they were growing up. Becoming involved with BBBS and H.O.P.E. Farm gave me a second chance.

I also wanted my three grandsons to be around other kids they might not otherwise get to know. My grandsons come from two-parent suburban families, and their lives mostly involve school, sports, band, and hanging out at the mall. I'm pleased that they have all these things in their lives, but I felt they needed to meet some other people who aren't so lucky. They also needed to see that, with or without those advantages, people are all the same inside. Kamerron and Cameron came from two of the poorest and most crime-infested areas of Fort Worth. By the end of the trip, though, there wasn't much difference between what any of the kids said, did, or ate. They were simply friends who cared about each other.

Although the main goal of our trip was to have fun, there were certain things I wanted all the boys to learn, and a few things that I required of them. Everyone had to keep a daily journal; take pictures; look people in the eye; say "thank you"; and write personal thank-you notes when we were given special attention or when the service we received was exceptional. This often meant getting people's names and business cards. It helped that the Embassy Suites hotels—where we stayed most of the time—had just started a program called Catch Me at My Best, which allowed any guest to recognize an employee by filling out a card and writing a personal note.

Looking people in the eye is important because it's a basic ingredient of self-esteem, and having high self-esteem is a key ingredient of success. The two boys from H.O.P.E. Farm had no problem looking people in the eye from the beginning, because Gary had trained them to do it. My grandsons and their friends had to learn this habit, but they came around quickly.

I discovered long ago that if something isn't recorded—either visually or on paper—then it can all too easily be forgotten. I felt that our trip would be more memorable, and the boys would remember it better and longer, if they each kept a journal. That's why I required them—as well as each of us adults—to write in journals each day. I reinforced this in two ways. First, I told the boys that the person who had the best journal and the most pictures would be formally recognized at the end of the trip with an extra dessert, something they all agreed was a fantastic idea. I also gave everyone on the trip (including each adult) a per diem of $10 on game days and $15 on non-game days—but for anyone to receive his per diem, he had to stay current with his journal. As a result, no one fell behind for very long.

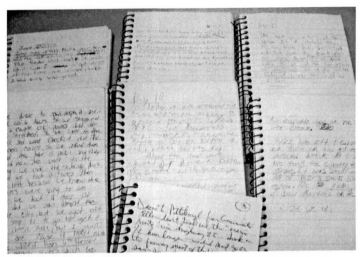

A look inside some of our journals.

By June of 2005, we had a starting lineup and a game plan. We would all gather in Fort Lauderdale, then head to Atlanta, Washington, DC, Cincinnati, Pittsburgh, Philadelphia, New York, Boston, Milwaukee, and Chicago—and then back to our respective hometowns.

On June 10, 2005, after almost a year of planning and preparation, our trip began.

Lesson 9
Say "Thank You"

The two greatest words in the English language are "thank you."

People like it when you say those words in writing. But they're even more powerful when you say them face to face.

I say "thank you" to my employees often. I say it promptly and loudly. In e-mails (and sometimes in snail mail letters, too) I use big letters and multiple bright colors. Most importantly, I use people's names.

People like to be acknowledged—but, even more, they like to be thanked—for their efforts and for their results. I have found that, like laughter, recognition and "thank you" are universal.

I've made it a practice to say thanks by e-mail every day. My business in Pakistan is 18,000 miles from Texas, and 10 hours ahead of us. If I send a "thank you" e-mail after skipping two days in a row, I'll receive this response: "Tom, we're glad you are back."

Lesson 10
Write Personal Notes

Writing a personal note is one of the most underused forms of positive communication—yet it is extremely easy to practice. In fact, writing personal notes is so effective that it should be taught in school, especially business classes.

Many people won't hesitate to write a letter to a corporate executive because of their company's poor service. But few take the time to acknowledge excellent service or to say "thank you" in writing for a job well done—even when someone goes well beyond the call of duty.

Let me give you three examples of how effective these notes can be.

Recently I had a meeting with the head of a growing search engine optimization company and several of his staff. After the meeting, I wrote each person a personal note, thanking them and commenting on the meeting. In response, the company president wrote me, telling me that the notes I had sent him and his staff were so powerful that he would be following the practice himself from then on.

The second example occurred in a class I taught in the University of North Texas's MBA program (where I teach many of the lessons in this book). One of my students was an elderly professor who taught marketing logistics. After the class, I sent him a note, thanking him for taking the time to attend, and asking if he could offer any advice for how I might improve it. He replied by saying that in 40 years of teaching, he had not received a note like mine before—and that he, too, was going to adopt the practice.

Third, recently I was selected to give a presentation to the heads of Freddie Mac in Washington, DC. To prove a point, I needed a copy of a tracking report we used at Associates many years before. I called on some of the company's other former employees to see if they had kept copies. Within 24 hours I had *three* different copies from three different former managers on my desk. All three had kept copies of the report, because I had written them personal notes about it 15 years ago, recognizing and appreciating them for their results.

An upbeat, sincere personal note can mean more to the recipient than almost anything else you can do. I've found this to be true in every country I've worked in—with big and small businesses, with nonprofits, and outside the workplace as well.

Yes, writing notes takes time, but the payoff is tremendous.

Lesson 11
The Power of Recognition

Recognition is one of the least-used motivators—yet it is the most powerful motivational tool in the world, bar none.

It's as universally appreciated as a smile, yet most people don't understand how to use it.

Recognition works miracles because it is personal, it is specific, and it can be saved and remembered.

I learned early in life that positive recognition for something you did makes you want to do it again. I still remember the time when my high school assistant principal saw me pick up a piece of paper and throw it in the garbage. He called me over, explained that what I did was important, and told me he appreciated it. From then on, for the past 50 years, I've picked up trash on the sidewalk as I walk.

For recognition to be effective, it has to have five qualities. First, it must be sincere. Second, it can't be used with the word "but" or "however" (as in, "You did a good job with the Bolinas project, but you could have done better."). Third, it should refer to specific things the person did, not just be a general "attaboy." Fourth, it must be timely—i.e., soon after the person has completed the task or taken the action you're recognizing. Fifth, recognition is most effective when it is provided verbally *and* followed up with something visual or tangible, such as a personal note. To make recognition even more powerful, you can add this sixth quality: recognize people privately at first, and then publicly afterward.

When I taught third graders at an Adopt-a-School program in Dallas, I drew a star on a student's paper next to each math problem they solved correctly. It wasn't long before they all worked to receive this recognition. Seeing their smiles when I walked into their classroom told me that this simple form of recognition had a profound effect on them.

On our baseball trip, the boys had a wonderful opportunity to practice the art of recognizing others. Embassy Suites' Catch Me at My Best program encouraged guests to tell management whenever an employee did a good job. Each room in each Embassy Suites hotel had a "We Appreciate You" card for guests to complete. The boys regularly filled out these cards and turned them in as we checked out. The people they wrote about in their notes were always very appreciative. Some, like Aida Gonzales, a front desk clerk at the Embassy Suites in New York, cried when the boys gave her their "We Appreciate You" card.

Lesson 12
Brag Books

If you respect your employees, care about them, and communicate clearly with them, they will do the same with your customers. And if your customers feel respected, cared about, and clearly communicated with, they will take good care of the company by buying its products or services. Over the past 40 years I have seen this approach work in large companies, small startups, and nonprofits.

One of the most effective (and popular) things I do is encourage each employee to keep a Brag Book. This is a simple, inexpensive three-ring binder with plastic sleeves in which they keep letters, cards, and e-mails complimenting their work. Because ownership is very important, I ask each employee to put their name, and a special cover of their choice, on the front of their binder.

Brag Books give employees a way to organize their accomplishments and compliments, which they then show to their families, coworkers, and friends. We don't need to coax folks into keeping these Brag Books. When given the opportunity (and the proper encouragement), people naturally save compliments, recommendations, and positive words.

Although many companies talk about how much they value their employees, in practice many don't actually sit down with each employee to review their performance, thank them for their results, and/or go over their goals. I know how important such meetings are, so in my company we also give each employee a log for tracking visits from their superiors. Each person keeps this log in their Brag Book. Every time one of an employee's superiors visits the employee's office, for any reason, they are required to sit down with that employee and review their Brag Book for a couple of minutes. The superior is also required to sign and date the employee's visitor log.

This has immediate, powerful, and positive effects on the employee. It also makes their superiors more aware of their achievements. As a result, they give employees more praise, which in turn encourages them to do an even better job. This arrangement also encourages supervisors to focus on and promote positive behavior, rather than just criticize failures and mistakes.

Brag Books are especially valuable in performance reviews, when each employee and their supervisor can view tangible evidence of the employee's accomplishments.

The log of superiors' visits also has another function. Upper management can review each employee's visitor log to make sure they are getting the right amount of attention from their immediate boss.

When I was at Associates, I visited our office in Wheeling, West Virginia and asked one employee if I could see her Brag Book. She responded, "Do you want to see both of them?" She had worked there for 21 years and had put together two huge Brag Books that weighed 10 pounds each. By the time she retired, she probably had a four-volume set.

Chapter 5
Opening Day

The first game on our schedule was in Miami, where the world-champion Marlins were to play our Texas Rangers. We were guests of businessman Norman Rales, a minority owner of the Marlins who had previously owned the Rangers for four years during the 1980s. Norman and I met in 1995 as a result of a misunderstood business arrangement between his company and Associates. This face-to-face meeting, which he requested, was one of the most fortunate experiences of my life. Over the 15 years since then, I have learned a great deal from Norman about mentoring. In fact, much of what he taught me appears in some of the lessons in this book.

Norman's story could only have happened in America. In 1930, when Norman was six, he and his sister were placed in a Jewish orphanage in Manhattan, where they grew up in secure but Spartan conditions. On Norman's 18th birthday he was given five dollars, escorted to the door, and told, "Go on your way—the world is yours." It's hard to imagine more modest beginnings. Within a few years, though, Norman had moved to Pittsburgh and established a very successful home improvement business. In the 1960s he moved again, to Washington, DC, where he launched a series of extremely profitable business ventures. By 1970 he was a multimillionaire. Today, at age 86, he's a well-known and widely respected philanthropist.

I learned early in life how important it is to prepare for any trip, meeting, or encounter by either making a dry run or showing up well in advance. So I arrived in Fort Lauderdale the day before everyone else did, to make certain that everything was in order.

Everything that we humans could control—the hotel, the rental van, and tickets to the game—was ready and waiting for us. But a terrible weather forecast awaited us as well. Arlene, the very first hurricane of the season, was headed toward south Florida. The weatherman told us to expect rain all day the following day—and for several days after that.

The next morning a light rain began to fall, and by 11 a.m. it had turned into a steady downpour. I drove to the airport, where I learned that, because of new rules after 9/11, I needed to get special approval to meet my grandsons at their gates. I also had to figure out how to meet planes from Louisville, Pittsburgh, and Dallas at about the same time.

My cell phone started ringing at 11:00 a.m. with the information that the flights from Pittsburgh (Matt, Sam, and Jimmy), Louisville (Andy and Spencer), and Dallas (Gary, Mike, Cameron, Kamerron, and Jake) were being kept on the ground because of the weather in Fort Lauderdale. Several calls from the boys' parents soon followed. You can imagine what was going through my mind. *Is this an omen? Will we face rain in every city? None of the stadiums has a roof except the new one in Milwaukee. Just what do you do with seven boys when it's raining?*

Eventually all three flights took off, and I learned that all three would arrive at roughly the same time—about three hours late. This meant we'd leave the airport two hours before the game was scheduled to begin. Not that there was much hope for a game, which looked like a rainout. I reminded myself that sometimes you just have to have faith.

The flights arrived; I was able to get through security to meet the planes; and all eleven of us eventually met up at the baggage claim.

The boys looked like they were on their way to compete in a wrestling match or soccer game. They all had big carry-on bags around their shoulders, MP3 players with earplugs, long hair, and sloppily fitting clothes. Everyone had a big smile—not because of me, but because, after flying through a huge rainstorm, they were very glad to be on the ground.

We were ready for some baseball—but outside it was raining cats and dogs. No, rhinos and elephants.

We drove to the Embassy Suites, checked in, and took a few minutes to unpack. Then I called the team together to go over the game plan for the trip—and to explain what we would do if the rain continued. I began by outlining the ground rules for the boys:

- I'd pay for all their expenses.

- Each boy (and each adult) would receive $10 spending money on game days and $15 on non-game days.

- All the boys would be treated exactly the same.

- Each boy—and each adult—received a journal, pens, and a camera for recording their activities each day.

- Everyone, including every adult, was expected to keep his journal current. To receive his per diem, each person had to show me that he had written in his journal the previous day.

- The boys could call their parents or guardians once per day.

- In each hotel we'd have three two-room suites, each with a living room and a bedroom. Three people would sleep in each suite (the third on a rollaway bed or on the convertible couch in the living room). We would shift roommates every other night, so that everyone would eventually room with everyone else.

- Whenever one of us was given great service, I expected him to get the name and address of the person who provided it, so he could send a thank-you note.

- We would have fun.

I also explained that if tonight's game were rained out, we'd simply have dinner at the hotel and go to bed early, because we had a 7 a.m. flight to Atlanta the next morning.

As I finished saying this, a huge clap of thunder shook the hotel. We all looked out the window at the sheets of rain. "*If* the game is rained out?" my grandson Sam asked.

Mike Meyer is the bearer of bad news about the Florida weather.

I was disappointed by how the trip had begun, but the boys weren't fazed at all. They were in a hotel with a big indoor pool, exercise equipment, clean towels, several restaurants, and people calling them "mister" and carrying their bags. As far as they were concerned, who needed baseball games?

Since Cameron had a video camera, we made him the official videographer for the trip. He was happy to shoulder this responsibility, and he turned out to be a talented camera-man. His first video clip of the trip showed all of us (except Cameron) in our suite's living room, smiling and waving, with torrential rain and bent-over palm trees in the background.

I hoped the weather wasn't an omen of things to come.

Lesson 13
It's Easier to Prepare Than Repair

We can save ourselves—and our customers—lots of time, money, and difficulties if we prepare properly.

Soon after I began working in the lending business, I learned that a loan that was properly made had a 98% chance of being fully collected. The large-scale failure of lenders to do this one obvious piece of preparation—properly qualifying potential borrowers—caused the worldwide financial meltdown of 2008, removing trillions of dollars from the economy. (Here's a tip for lending professionals: the time to ask a customer how they will pay back a loan is before they have your money.)

Preparation means laying out what you want to accomplish, how you want to accomplish it, where you want to accomplish it, the time-frame in which you want to accomplish it, who you want to accomplish it with, and how you will know it's been accomplished. This process requires that you ask other people—and yourself—a lot of questions. It also requires lots of practice and walk-throughs.

Sometimes preparation can be simple. At the beginning of my career, when my boss flew in for a meeting, part of my job was to pick him up at the airport and deliver him to his hotel. I always did a practice run the day before. As a result, I knew about—and was able to avoid—road closures, traffic bottlenecks, airport parking issues, and other potential problems. I always got my boss to the hotel in time and without incident.

Sometimes these little things can mean a small step ahead of your competition. They certainly did for me.

Most of us have heard horror stories of business people who didn't prepare in some simple way, and delivered the chairman of the board to the wrong meeting or showed up late to give an important talk. I've watched lots of young, talented executives get passed over for promotions because they failed to properly prepare by attending to small but important details.

Lesson 14
Sometimes You Just Need to Have Faith

Sometimes you can plan, prepare, and execute everything perfectly—yet things go wrong because of events that are entirely out of your control. A grounder takes a bad hop.

A ballgame gets rained out. A flight is cancelled because of mechanical problems. A terrorist flies a plane into a skyscraper.

During these times, the most positive—and most practical—thing you can do is have faith. This means not worrying over those things you can't control. (After all, if you can't control them, what good will worrying do?) It also means doing the one thing you *can* control: following (and, if necessary, creating) a Plan B.

Chapter 6
Prayers, Hope, and Superman

My cell phone rang. It was Norman Rales. He said, "Tom, it looks like tonight's game isn't going to be played. But I want you, Gary, and the boys to drive to the stadium anyway. I'll meet you inside Entrance 14."

We piled into the van, the rain pounding us and the wind whipping at our clothing.

The drive to Sun Life Stadium (which then was called Pro Player Stadium) only took 20 minutes, but in those 20 minutes I must have said five silent prayers for our safety. I also hoped for some kind of miracle—that the rain would stop, or that we would somehow have a memorable evening in spite of it. It had been falling for eight straight hours, and all indications were that things would get worse, not better.

But, just as we entered the ballpark, the rain slowed to a drizzle, then stopped. The eleven of us looked at each other with a glimmer of hope.

Norman was waiting for us with a big smile. He shook hands with each of us and led the way toward the owners' box.

Norman and the boys hit it off almost immediately. Norman knows three U.S. presidents personally, yet talks at the level of the average person. He understands how much can be achieved through simple, common interactions. He's also always watching, listening, and teaching.

Within minutes, he set an example for the boys. The usher at the entrance to the front row of seats was a young man who was physically and mentally challenged. Norman touched his shoulder and said, "Young man, tell us how to get to our seats."

The young man's face broke into a big smile. He pointed to the front row and said, "You all go right through there to your seats."

"Thank you," Norman said emphatically. He pulled a silver dollar from his pocket and gave it to the young man. He had made another friend.

The point was not lost on any of the boys. All of them understood that Norman knew exactly where our seats were and didn't need the young man's help. But his actions reminded them that when you allow someone to do their job, you build their self-esteem. (The silver dollar was a bonus. Norman usually has a pocketful of these and hands them out often.)

To my surprise, the field was in excellent condition, even though it had rained all day. The rain continued to hold off, and the game started on time.

Andy's friend Spencer described our seats as "spectacular." It was an accurate description. We were right behind the Marlins' dugout, only a few feet from the players. We could hear much of their talk throughout the game, and occasionally one would look at us and nod, or flash us a quick smile.

The boys also showed a deep appreciation for the Marlins' cheerleaders. As we watched the young women perform, one grandson—I no longer remember which one, but he appeared to speak for all the boys—said, very loudly, "Grandpa, you have made my day." All the boys took lots of pictures of the players, the cheerleaders, the stadium, the cheerleaders, the scoreboard, and the cheerleaders.

We not only had the best seats in the house, but at times we felt the game was being played just for us. Because of the weather, very few fans had turned out. Some of us were able to stand up to get a better look without blocking other people's view. The boys did this a lot with the cheerleaders.

Sometime during the game I discovered that this was the first time that Andy, Cameron, and Kamerron were inside a Major League Baseball stadium. Up until now, they had only watched Major League Baseball on TV and gone to live Minor League games.

The game, the players, and the cheerleaders weren't the only attractions. Norman introduced us to the Marlins' majority owner and gave us all Marlins shirts. The boys got to see and (for a few seconds each) wear the Marlins' 2003 World

Series ring, which looks like a belt buckle and is valued at $50,000. We also got a couple of baseballs from the Marlins' ball boy. I had hoped for one for each of the boys, but the ball boy must have been told to conserve them, because he handed out very few—even though we begged and pleaded for them. Meanwhile, the Rangers' ball boy, across the field, handed out balls like candy.

Jeffrey Loria, owner of the Florida Marlins, flashes the Marlins' 2003 World Series ring.

The boys also received a few words from Norman about how life and baseball are similar. In the fifth inning, Carlos Delgado hit a long ball off the wall. The center fielder re-covered the ball but missed the cutoff man, which allowed Delgado to go to third base. A few minutes later, Delgado scored on a sacrifice grounder. As he jogged back to the dugout, Norman said to the boys, "Did you see what happened? Sometimes mistakes don't show up on the box score. The center fielder didn't get charged with an error for missing the cutoff man. But it cost the team just as much as dropping a ball or overthrowing the first baseman. It might even cost the team the game." Norman paused and let this sink in. Then he said, "In life, sometimes our mistakes aren't noticeable to others—but they still make a difference. They can mean less achievement in school, or higher costs and lower profits in business. Just because someone doesn't see your mistake and write it down doesn't mean the mistake won't have negative consequences." It's often hard to tell with adolescent boys, but it looked to me like they got Norman's message.

Norman also told this true story about himself and his son Mitch. In 1959, Norman and his family lived in Pittsburgh. Back then, kids in Pittsburgh had two big heroes: Superman and the Pirates' second baseman, Bill Mazeroski. One morning, as Norman was leaving for work, he asked Mitch, who was eight, what he was watching on TV. "Superman," Mitch said. Norman replied, "Son, you know I'm the real Superman." Mitch said emphatically, "No, you're not." So Norman asked, "What would it take to prove to you that I'm actually Superman?" Mitch thought about it a bit and said, "I'll believe you're Superman if you bring Bill Mazeroski home for lunch."

Normally this would be quite a tall order. But it so happened that Norman had a meeting with the Pirates' owner, Joe Brown, that morning. Norman wanted his home improvement company to sponsor some of the Pirates' games;

he was also interested in hiring some of the players to serve as spokesmen for his business. (Believe it or not, in 1959 the average annual salary of a Major League Baseball player was only about $6000, so many players were happy to moonlight.) When he raised the possibility to Joe Brown, Brown said, "It's okay by me as long as it doesn't interfere with any games or practices. Talk to whomever you want. In fact, Bill Mazeroski and his wife are sitting outside my office. You can go talk to them now."

Norman left the office, introduced himself to Mazeroski and his wife, and, after a few minutes of conversation, hired him as a spokesman. Evidently part of the deal also involved Mazeroski going back to Norman's home for lunch.

You can imagine Mitch's reaction when Norman returned home with Bill Mazeroski in tow. Today, 45 years later, Mitch still refers to his dad as "the real Superman." (By the way, the very next year, the Pirates won the World Series, defeating the Yankees after seven games. The Pirates scored the winning run in the bottom of the ninth inning with a home run by—of course—Bill Mazeroski.)

Mitch also learned a thing or two from his father about building a successful business. He and his brother Steven are the co-founders and majority stockholders of Danaher Corporation, one of the country's most profitable businesses. Mitch also routinely appears on the Forbes 400 list of the world's richest people, with a net worth of well over $2 billion.

By the end of the Rangers-Marlins game, all of the boys felt pretty rich themselves. They got to see a grand slam, dozens of Major League players, and—perhaps most important to these 13-to-16-year-old boys—some very pretty girls. And, miraculously, not a drop of rain fell throughout all nine innings (though it began raining again as we headed back to our hotel). Oh, by the way, the Marlins won the game 12-5 against our Rangers. But none of the boys cared.

As we left the stadium, my grandson Sam looked at me and said, "I sure am glad you're my grandpa." When I heard that, I felt pretty rich, too.

Lesson 15
Watch and Listen Actively

In business, mentoring, and life, it's important to watch and listen—especially when the people you're observing don't think you are.

Sometimes you need to wait for the right moment to get your message or lesson across. When now isn't the right time, you can put what you saw or heard in your pocket. Then you can bring it out later, when the person is paying attention, receptive, and ready to learn from it.

Sometimes being quiet is the best mentoring skill of all. There are times when it's best to observe but say nothing, and let the person learn through their own experience.

Lesson 16
Help People Be Successful

One of the best and fastest ways to help people build self-esteem is to allow them to do the job we assign them to do.

We can do this by making certain that they have the right tools, the proper instructions, and the necessary follow up—including any needed one-to-one guidance and correction. Then we can catch them doing things right, and acknowledge them.

When this process is correctly used, nothing works better or faster to create self-confidence and productivity.

Gary Randle does this every day with dozens of boys. Norman Rales did it at a baseball game just by allowing a young man to guide us to our seats.

Chapter 7
Early Arrivals and Bottomless Bellies

I make it a point to get to places early. To me, making someone wait for you is the height of arrogance. My rule is to arrive at a meeting 20-30 minutes before it begins, and at an airport 90 minutes before departure time.

Before we turned in that first night, I made it clear to everyone that we would all follow my early-arrival rule throughout our trip. To my surprise, there was no massive protest, only a couple of grumbles.

One added benefit of getting places early is that you often meet new people—and there's time to talk with them. That's what happened to us at the Fort Lauderdale airport the next morning. As we waited to board our plane, I recognized Carlton Sheets, who has sold more real estate over national television than any realtor in history. I introduced myself,

Gary, Mike, and the boys to him, and told him about our trip. Sheets was gracious and happy to talk. He treated all the boys as adults, which built their self-esteem an additional notch. I was pleased that all the boys treated him respectfully as well.

The young men were impressed with the Delta plane, which had seven seats per row. They also received special attention from the flight attendants, who were obviously very experienced with adolescent male passengers, and made sure they would be happy and compliant.

We take lots of things for granted, including air travel. To me, our flight to Atlanta was just another trip, and I spent the flight reading and napping. But here's what Kamerron wrote in his journal:

> *My favorite memory of the flight was looking out the window and seeing all the ponds and small lakes. I really loved being above the clouds and going through them.*

After two hours in the air we arrived in Atlanta, where we collected our bags and got on the Embassy Suites shuttle. It was too early to check into our rooms, so the shuttle-bus driver took us to the airport's Ruby Tuesday for lunch.

If you ever plan to travel with a group of adolescent American boys, here's a word to the wise: your biggest expense will be food. At each meal, every one of the boys ate like they hadn't been fed in days. I let everyone order whatever they wanted, but I quickly learned that, except at breakfast, every boy would usually order one of three things: steak and a baked potato; a hamburger and fries; or either a steak or a hamburger with a baked potato *and* fries. Pizza was a distant fourth choice. In 21 days with these boys, I gained 20 pounds—and it felt as if 10 of these were through osmosis, from sitting next to these eating machines.

Two policewomen in uniform were seated a few tables away. After we finished eating, I walked to their table, introduced myself, and asked if they'd spend a few minutes talking with the boys. They were happy to. It turned out they worked for the airport's bomb-detection unit. They spent nearly half an hour talking about their jobs, the importance of education, and how they had worked their way up into this elite unit. We documented the session with a picture of the group, and they invited us to visit their headquarters on our next visit to the Atlanta airport.

If it sounds like I constantly introduce myself to strangers, you're right. It's true, I'm not afraid to strike up a conversation with someone who seems interesting. But on this trip I did it much more than usual, because I wanted the boys to engage with a variety of professionals, to get comfortable with people they didn't know, to hear success stories from people working in a variety of different careers, and to see for themselves how everyone can succeed with hard work, education, and a smart plan.

After lunch we got back on the Embassy Suites shuttle, headed to the hotel, and checked in.

Everyone who worked for this hotel, from the shuttle-bus driver to the front-desk receptionist, was very friendly and helpful. No one seemed to mind that Gary, Mike, and I were herding a throng of noisy adolescent boys. The boys appreciated the good service, too, and wrote many thank-you notes.

Tom and one of the police officers who provided on-the-spot mentoring at Ruby Tuesday in Atlanta.

After an hour of rest, we headed out for an afternoon game between the Braves and the Oakland Athletics at Turner Field. Here we were the guests of another of my friends, John Markos, who had arranged for us to sit in his company's luxury suite. I expected the boys to be in awe of the new stadium, the giant $80 million scoreboard, the cushioned seats inside, and the covered seats outside. They weren't. What excited them was the endless supply of free food. We had just eaten a huge meal two hours earlier, but all of the boys were ready for more.

Here's how three of the boys described the game in their journals:

Andy: *It was awesome! We were in a suite with free food. I ate during the entire game.*

Spencer: *The seats were awesome. We were in the VIP box. There were free hot dogs, chicken strips, and pizza.*

Kamerron: *We got something special. We got box seats and got to eat free food. We ate pizza, chicken, popcorn, and hot dogs.*

The game itself was almost a non-event for the boys. (The Braves won, 5-3.) After all, how can you watch a game closely when you're eating all the time?

After the game, however, Cameron asked some questions that created a perfect teaching moment: "How do people earn the money to buy a baseball team (like Norman Rales), or afford a suite like the one we were in today (like John Markos)? And how does anyone get the money to buy stock?" I briefly outlined Norman and John's careers, and told Cameron we'd have a discussion later about what he would need to do to get started in a career of his own. Knowing that we'd soon be in New York City, I also said that he'd get to learn more about the stock market soon.

When we got back to the hotel, there was time to swim, watch TV, and talk. Everyone was in a festive mood. We had been to two Major League Baseball games in two days, and at each game we had been treated royally.

Everyone agreed that we should send special thank-you notes to both John Markos and Norman Rales. After some discussion, we decided to do more than that. For each one, we put together a shadow box that included a thank-you note, a game ticket, and a baseball autographed by all the boys. Norman and John later agreed that these were major-league gifts.

One of the shadow boxes we created for John Markos and Norman Rales.

By now Gary, Mike, and I had learned several things about the boys. First, they were all well mannered, smart, and respectful with adults. Second, they followed instructions well. Third, they loved to eat. Fourth, they didn't sleep much. Fifth, as the boys got to know one another, we watched their differences melting away. At least for adolescent boys, baseball and food remove the divisions caused by race, religion, politics, fears, problems, and stress.

Mike Meyer, Bob Meyer, Gary Randle, and Tom Slone with one of the shadow boxes.

Lesson 17
Become a Connector

People call me a connector. I connect people to each other so that they can help one another. Often, in the process, one of them helps me, too. That's not the reason why I connect them, but it's a very common outcome.

Being a connector requires you to take a sincere interest in other people. You need to genuinely want to help them, for no other reason than it's the right thing to do. You also need to put other people's needs ahead of your own wants.

Over the years, I have helped people connect in order to find jobs (and qualified employees), to build their businesses, and to solve practical problems. I have also made many friends in the process.

Being a connector feels good, too. As our great President Abraham Lincoln said, "When I do good, I feel good. When I do bad, I feel bad. That's my religion." There's nothing that makes me feel better than helping someone.

Here's one of the simplest and most effective techniques for being a connector: When you meet someone, get their business card or their name and contact information. Don't give them your own card yet; if you're asked for one, give them your contact information, but not your card. Then, as soon as you get back to your office, mail them your business card, along with a personal note. By doing this you have separated your card from all the other cards; and when you send your card with a personal note, you're more likely to be remembered. Try it—you'll like the results.

Lesson 18
Talk to Strangers

Over the past 40 years, being willing to talk to strangers has helped me—and many of those strangers—a great deal. It's also proven to me, time after time, that the world is much smaller than we imagine. Here is just one example.

I make several trips to Pakistan every year for the business I co-own there. In 2007, while I was in Islamabad, I decided to purchase carpets for our new home from a store that came highly recommended. I met the owner, Imran Khan, whose carpet business has been in his family for five generations. I was very pleased with both his products and his customer service. In fact, we became good friends, discussing the politics, culture, and business practices in Pakistan. I had just read and enjoyed *Hug Your Customers* by Jack Mitchell, so I sent him a copy.

A year later, a huge shareholder dispute occurred in my Pakistan business. It was big enough to make the national and international news, and received major coverage by the business press in Islamabad.

That fall, as I was having breakfast with Charles Pierson, the CEO of Big Brothers Big Sisters, he told me that Eric Stumberg, one of the BBBS board members from Austin, Texas, would soon take a hunting trip in Pakistan. He asked me to call Eric, which I did, even though we had never met. I introduced myself and told him that I would have executives from our facility in Islamabad call him so that he would have contacts in the country if any issues came up. I then called two of our key people in Islamabad and asked them to call Eric. I also sent Eric a copy of *Hug Your Customers*.

Two days later, Eric called to say that he had landed in Islamabad safely, and that he really appreciated my call, as well as the ones from our executive team. I said I was pleased to hear from him and wished him well.

A day later, I received another call from Eric. He told me he had been looking for carpets for his new home in Austin, and that he had met a friend of mine: Imran Khan. The two ended up chatting about me, and about *Hug Your Customers*.

Three hours later, I received a call from Imran. He explained that a friend of mine had been in his store and bought a lot of carpets. Imran also said that Eric would be hunting with one of the most influential Pakistani Americans in Pakistan—and that if Eric spoke to him, he could probably help me with my shareholder dispute.

Please remember that Pakistan is 18,000 miles (18 hours fight time) from Texas and there are over 1,500 carpet stores in this area of Pakistan. What are the odds of these three people *connecting*?

THINGS HAPPEN FOR A REASON.

I'm glad I made that call to a stranger.

Lesson 19
Honest Answers

Asking why is one of the best mentoring practices. When you ask someone to reflect on and explain the reasons for an action they took or a decision they made, this helps them understand the consequences of that action or decision more clearly. It also encourages them to make wiser choices in the future.

Letting others ask *you* why—and answering those questions fully and honestly—is equally important. Our first Little Brother continually asked questions about everything. This was a good thing in two ways: first, it meant he was curious and genuinely interested in the world, not just in himself; second, it showed that he trusted us.

It's especially important to explain to people why things are done a certain way, rather than just telling them to do it "because I said so." This gives them some ownership in the task—and it encourages them to excel, not merely comply.

After our visit to Wall Street (which you'll read about later in this book), all the boys—but especially Cameron—had all kinds of questions about wealth, how the stock market worked, and how they could earn money. Gary and I answered these questions as thoroughly as we could. That fall, Cameron wrote an excellent report about the stock market for school. In fact, I wrote him a letter complimenting him on it, and sent a copy to his principal.

Chapter 8
History 10, Baseball 6

Our next stop was Washington, DC. Our plan was to spend one day watching a Nationals game, and another visiting some of the many historical monuments that tell our nation's history.

In the morning we got up, packed, and left the hotel very early. The Nationals were playing a 1:00 p.m. game, and in order to get from Reagan Airport to our hotel, check in, and make it to the stadium on time, we needed to take a 6 a.m. plane from Atlanta.

Our flight to Washington left and arrived on time, and we made it to our hotel on schedule. We checked in, threw our bags in our suite, and headed for RFK Stadium.

The boys learned several lessons during our two days in Washington, and the first one came early on. Washington has a great subway system, the Metro, which stops only a block from the ballpark. I assigned Matt the tasks of guiding us from the Embassy Suites to the nearest Metro stop and getting us on the right train. He led us quickly to the stop and put us on the correct line—but in the wrong direction. We ended up not at RFK Stadium, but in suburban Virginia.

Jake, Tom, Jimmy, Sam, Gary, and Matt on the flight from Atlanta to Washington, DC.

Matt was hugely embarrassed at first, and very apologetic. As the oldest of the boys, he felt we expected him to be the most responsible and reliable. But Gary and I told him that we all make mistakes sometimes. We learn from them and continue forward. As my wife often says, "No one died—let's move on." So we got off the train, got on another going the opposite direction, and got to the stadium just as the game began.

Kamerron and Sam buy subway farecards for the Washington, DC Metro.

The ambiance at RFK Stadium was several steps down from that of our first two games. We had great seats, but they were out in the sun. It was the middle of a Washington summer afternoon, and the temperature was over 100 degrees. The stadium was old (not long afterward, it was replaced by the new Nationals Park); there were no cheerleaders in skimpy costumes; there was no free, all-you-can-eat food; and the concession stands, as one of the boys noted, "sucked." We had been spoiled by our first two outings. As another of the boys observed in his journal, *It was a very exciting game; however, we didn't have a suite.* The game *was* exciting even though the weather was so hot. The Nationals edged out Seattle 3-2, ending a four-game losing streak.

A very happy Jake with three young ladies in sexy costumes at RFK Stadium in Washington, DC.

One never knows when an opportunity to teach will appear—or, for that matter, when someone is ready to learn. But on the way back to our hotel from the ballpark, we had another one of those moments when everything aligned. The boys were tired and—no surprise—hungry. We got on the right train this time and were back above ground 15 minutes later, walking the few blocks to our hotel.

Suddenly I saw three coins in the gutter. I stopped and bent down to pick them up. "What are you doing?" one of the boys asked me. I held up what I had found: two pennies and a gold Susan B. Anthony dollar coin. "I just made some money," I told them. "And all I did to make it was pay attention. Keep your own eyes open, and you'll be surprised how much money you'll find, just sitting there right in front of you." I explained to them that I usually walk about six miles a day; as I do, I think, plan, and stay alert. If I see a coin or a bill (and I've found plenty of those, too), I pick it up. "You'd be surprised how much loot is left on the ground," I told them. "I average about $50 to $60 a year, just by keeping my eyes open."

The lesson was as much about staying alert as it was about finding dropped money. But the boys took both parts of the lesson to heart. Almost every morning for the rest of our trip, one of them would say, "Guess what I found yesterday, Mr. Tom? A dime." Or, "I found a quarter this morning, Grandpa."

This past summer (five years after the baseball trip), Matt visited us in Texas. He's now a junior at Slippery Rock University in Pennsylvania, where he is on the Dean's List. Frances and I took the opportunity to have a small get-together. We invited Bob, Gary, Mike, Cameron, and Kamerron. Bob, Gary, and Cameron (who is a now a freshman at the University of Texas at San Antonio) were able to attend. As you can imagine, the discussion centered on the baseball trip. Cameron is still focused on how to make money, and he told the group of 20+ people that, even today, when he walks with his friends and sees a coin on the ground, he picks it up, even though his friends laugh. He tells them, "Hey, I know a rich man who picks up money, and if it's good enough for him, it's good enough for me." Kids do as we do, not as we say—believe me, I know this for a fact.

Mike Meyer, Tom Slone, Gary Randle, and the crew outside RFK Stadium in Washington, DC.

Back to DC. After getting cleaned up, our group walked up the street to the Front Page Restaurant and Grill, whose walls were covered with newspaper front pages from the past hundred years. There were stories about World Wars I and II, an article about Harry Truman dropping the first atomic bomb, and another about the assassination of President Kennedy. Many of these headlines were entirely new information to the boys. Kids in most other countries know their history; our kids don't. This is one area where we are far behind most of the rest of the world.

We ate a huge meal consisting of, you guessed it, steak, baked potatoes, and French fries, and headed back to the Embassy Suites for a swim before going to bed.

The next morning we slept in until 7:00 a.m. (a late beginning for us), ate breakfast, and headed out to see some of the city's historic sights. There's no way you can see everything worthwhile in our nation's capital in a day, a week, or even a month, but we were able to visit some of its most important landmarks. We arranged for a large van with a guide so we could make the best use of our time. We started with the White House. Then we visited the Lincoln Memorial, where everyone took the time to read the Gettysburg Address. Those 256 words continue to have immense meaning today.

Mike Meyer, Gary Randle, Tom Slone, and the young men in front of the White House.

We have come a long way in our views on race and human rights since Lincoln's time, and even since the 60s—yet it was clear to Gary and me that Kamerron and Cameron didn't really understand what their forefathers went through. It never crossed their minds that, only two generations earlier, it would have been rare—and, in some parts of the country, impossible—for all of us to be on the same plane together, to eat at the same table, and to sleep in the same hotel rooms. Maybe we *should* take our equality for granted, because it's how God created us. But many of us who lived through a time when there was no equality still live with painful memories, grief, and regret. And today there is still more to do to ensure that equality is part of American life for many generations to come.

Spencer, Jake, Mike Meyer, Cameron, and Abe Lincoln.

Next we visited the Vietnam Memorial. Spencer looked up a family friend in the guide, and we found his name on the wall. Other visitors had left notes and flowers close by his name. As we stood in front of the wall, Spencer called his family and told them that one of his missions had been accomplished.

The boys were wide-eyed as we walked around the Korean War Memorial, where the nineteen steel soldiers looked intense and very real. We had our picture taken by the wall that offered this powerful reminder: "Freedom is not free."

We travelled to the new World War II Memorial, the Washington Monument, the Nurses Memorial in Arlington Cemetery, and several other sites. At many of these, the boys asked Gary, Mike, and me questions about our nation's history. This told me that our kids are willing to study history, if only we can make it more interesting than we do now—perhaps by making it more about people and less about dates. If our kids do learn history and take it to heart, maybe the next generation won't repeat all the mistakes their ancestors made.

At the end of that day, I was quite proud of the young men for several reasons: they demonstrated a great deal of respect; they reflected on everything they saw; they asked lots of good questions (especially Spencer about Vietnam); and they seemed to understand that freedom is earned, not given, and should never be taken for granted.

At the end of that day, on a scale of 1 to 10, the boys gave the previous day's baseball game a 6, and the historical tour a 10.

Now we had come to a short break in the trip. The boys would fly home to Louisville, Pittsburgh, and Dallas to check in with their families and get clean clothes. Then we would meet again, two days later, in Cincinnati.

Cameron, Kamerron, Andy, Spencer, Sam, Jimmy, and Jake had started out four days ago as strangers, but they were melding into a solid group of friends. I wasn't as positive about Matt, who stayed more to himself. I worried that he would turn into a loner for the rest of the trip—but my fears proved unfounded. The next day, when I got home to Fort Worth, Matt called to ask if he could bring a friend on the second leg of our journey. It was a huge thrill for me to have Matt ask, and of course I said yes.

I talked to each boy's parents or guardians, telling them what great young men they had raised. I explained that each boy always said "thank you," consistently used good manners, and was polite to all the people he met. In every case, the response I got was a variant of, "Are you sure you're talking about *our* boy?"

People often ask me why these boys acted differently with us than they did at home. I give them this answer:

- First, this trip was a new experience for them. They couldn't rely on their usual behavior because each situation was fresh and unexpected.

- Second, they were afraid. They had been told by their parents and guardians that they had better behave— and the boys knew they meant it.

- Third, on this trip, we adults acted differently around *them* than most of the adults they came in contact with every day. We were very clear about what we expected from them—and we expected that they would be courteous, mannered, and polite. Most of all, though, we respected them and their ideas, questions, and comments. Sometimes giving respect can make all the difference. I have been told that, as with love, you have to always give respect before you get it. On our trip, these boys were living proof that this statement is true.

Lesson 20
Opportunities

Over the years, I've come across more opportunities than I ever imagined possible, just by doing five things:

- Being an active listener.

- Putting other people's wants and desires ahead of my own.

- Acknowledging, recognizing, and thanking people consistently.

- Connecting people who need help in solving an issue with others who can help them.

- Following up to make certain progress is being made.

This doesn't mean that every opportunity should be pursued. It's important to be discerning, and to proceed thoughtfully and carefully. You need to understand the risks and the potential rewards. You also need to be aware of what things you can control and which ones you can't. And you need to understand your own strengths, weaknesses, and limits. (I know, for example, that my strength is people and my weakness is the numbers side of the business. Therefore, I never pursue an opportunity without getting the ongoing guidance of a numbers person.)

Lesson 21
It's Okay to Look Back at the Past; Just Don't Stare

My friend Doris Roberts, a comedian and actress who is best known for her role on "Everybody Loves Raymond," recently gave a speech to a university class with the title "It's Okay to Look Back—Just Don't Stare." It's a great theme and a wonderful lesson.

Looking at the past is often essential to success. When creating a plan, it's important to review past experiences and past results, so that you don't make the same mistakes that were made before. In fact, I sometimes tell people that having a great memory is just as beneficial as having a new idea. I've found that many of the things we used to do to create success get forgotten and replaced with new things, which may or may not work better.

In my company, before we decide to do anything big and new, I remind people to look at what has worked before for us, and to see if any of it can be adapted to make it current. When it can, it often creates excellent results and big savings in costs.

But it's also possible to put too much emphasis on the past. Many things *are* different today, and some require different approaches and solutions. What often works is to keep long-standing, tried-and-true principles, but to apply them in a new way or with a new twist.

Lesson 22
Quality vs. Quantity

Early in my life, I learned that *quantity never leads to quality*—but *quality ultimately leads to quantity.* The more things you do right, the more things you have time to do.

The credit crisis we faced in 2008 can be traced back to people choosing quantity over quality. "Let's book as many mortgage loans as we can, as fast as we can. We can go back and document them correctly later." Yet often these loans were *never* correctly documented. Many lenders didn't do the necessary checking, either, and simply let the loans slide through. No one kept track or corrected mistakes. Eventually everyone became so lax, and got so focused on quantity, that they created a trillion-dollar problem.

In both business and mentoring, we need to stress quality again and again before we even think about pushing for quantity. A new employee should initially be encouraged to do quality work, and be recognized and rewarded for it (and penalized for not doing it). Only when quality work has become their habit should they be encouraged to focus on increasing their productivity.

It's the same with raising or mentoring kids. If we keep our kids busy with lots of activities, but give them little meaningful one-to-one time, the whole family could face major problems as the kids grow older.

Chapter 9
Our Great Ohio Meetup

We met up again in Cincinnati. Since all my grand-kids lived reasonably close to that city, we decided to make our outing there into a family gathering.

As a result, we had a gathering of 19 people—enough to field two actual baseball teams. My daughter-in-law Ellen drove Matt, Sam, and Matt's girlfriend from Pittsburgh, about three and a half hours away. My two daughters, Carrie and Kellye, drove Andy and my four granddaughters (Kacey, Samantha, Chrissy, and Katelyn) from Louisville, a two-and-a-half-hour trip. Spencer came with his dad and sister. Gary, Kamerron, and Cameron arrived together by plane. Mike Meyer's dad Bob replaced Mike, who stayed in Dallas to keep an eye on our business. Mike's son Jake also left our entourage.

To accommodate this human menagerie, we needed six suites at the Embassy Suites. We also needed 19 tickets to the Cincinnati Reds game. Luckily we didn't need a bunch of rental cars because we were close enough to the ballpark to walk to the game.

Bob and I caught an early flight in order to get to Cincinnati a few hours before everyone else. We made sure the cars, rooms, and tickets were ready when the others arrived. To our surprise, there was a mix-up in the number of rooms and who was with whom. But after a little discussion everything got sorted out.

Bob is a huge fan of both baseball and kids. He's quiet, professional, and always a gentleman. He felt he had a lot to offer the boys. But mentoring is a funny thing: you have to wait for the right time and place, when people are receptive and paying attention. We had a few of those moments on this second leg of our trip, but Bob would have liked to have had many more.

Our hotel was in Kentucky, just across the Ohio River from Great American Ball Park, so we all walked across the suspension bridge to the park.

The game was good and the ballpark was great, with clean, air-conditioned eating areas—and fantastic hot dogs. The Reds lost to St. Louis, but everyone in the park seemed to have a great time anyway. The game was a pitching gem—the first one we'd seen on our trip. Neither pitcher gave up a run until the ninth inning. The one other highlight involved fashion: Bob tried to make his shirt match the ushers' by spilling mustard all over his.

Waiting for the game to begin at Great American Ball Park in Cincinnati.

After the game, we walked back across the bridge to swim and relax at the hotel. To my surprise, when I got to my room, I found a huge basket of Cincinnati Reds memorabilia waiting for me. Attached to it was a note from the hotel management, apologizing for their earlier mix-up. Here was an example of a company not just meeting their customers' expectations, but exceeding them. As Gary, Bob, and I handed out Reds caps to the boys, we used the Embassy Suites' extra efforts to make a point: don't just get by, excel.

By now the boys knew the drill. They got out their pens and wrote thank-you notes.

The hotel's apology also provided me with a second teaching moment. I explained that when you make a mistake or disappoint someone, you shouldn't ignore it. Instead, you need to acknowledge it, correct it, and make amends with a note and/or a gift. This isn't just the right thing to do; it's also good business. I've never forgotten that gift basket, and since then I've told literally hundreds of people about the great service that the folks at Embassy Suites provide.

The next morning, after breakfast, I said goodbye to most of the group. Spencer's father went back with his daughter later that day. Carrie, Kellye, and my granddaughters drove back to Louisville. Just before they left, I heard, for the umpteenth time, "I wish I could go with you guys."

The rest of us, including my daughter-in-law Ellen and Matt's girlfriend, planned to drive to Pittsburgh in a mini-caravan of three cars. My original plan was to take the interstate, but Ellen, who had agreed to lead the way, said she knew a short cut.

It turned out to be nothing of the sort. We hadn't driven more than an hour when we knew we were in trouble. When we figured this out, we were on a two-lane road in the middle of nowhere. Ellen stopped and made a u-turn; the two cars behind her did the same. Boy, did she catch grief for this. The boys said it was "a typical blonde move."

It took us five and a half hours instead of the usual three and a half to get to Pittsburgh. But we did get to see some very small towns, lots of cars with two-tone paint jobs (a hood or a door with a different color than the rest of the car), and many front porches featuring washing machines and sofas.

We found our way to the Embassy Suites close to the airport and checked in. Now Cameron and Kamerron were rooming with me. This gave Cameron the chance to ask me some very sharp questions about stocks: *Where do you buy them, and from whom? Where do people get the money they invest? What happens to a stock once you own it?* I explained the steps and process once more, and reminded him that he'd learn much more when we reached New York City.

By now it was clear to me that Cameron was very articulate, and had the ability to become a leader. But it was equally obvious that he needed a strong male influence in his life. He also needed to learn to practice discipline and channel his energy. I was very glad that he had Gary. In the days that followed, I spent a lot of time talking to Cameron about the things he could do that would make people proud of him.

My other current roommate, Kamerron, had recently acquired a new nickname from Gary: Campy. The name came from Roy Campanella, the great catcher for the Brooklyn Dodgers in the 40s and 50s. Campanella was one of the first players to break Major League Baseball's color barrier. The name Campy fit Kamerron perfectly: he was built like Campanella and had the same optimistic demeanor and infectious smile.

In each city we visited, I encouraged the boys to try the local specialties. Most of the time, they ignored my suggestions. (In Atlanta, for example, no one but me ordered grits.) But I had a hunch that things would be different in Pittsburgh, where a famous local dish is steak salad: steak and French fries mixed with lettuce, hard-boiled eggs, and cheese, all covered with warm Italian dressing.

My hunch was very wrong. All the boys ordered the steak salad minus the lettuce, dressing, cheese, and eggs.

When the waitress asked Cameron how he wanted his steak cooked, he thought for a few seconds and said, "The one that comes just before burnt."

I was very impressed with Pittsburgh's new stadium, PNC Park, and with the city in general, which is quite beautiful and clean. If you have visions of an old steel-mill town covered in soot, you need to visit the new Pittsburgh. It's living proof that with the right focus, plan, and execution, many good things can happen.

The game itself was a win for the Pirates (11-4 over the Nationals), only their second win in their last nine games. We also saw the Pirates' manager get thrown out. (He had rushed out of the dugout after a player was called out at the plate.)

Watching the Pirates and the Nationals play at PNC Park in Pittsburgh.

After the game, I suggested that we stop at Kings Restaurant for their famous apple pie and cinnamon ice cream, something my wife Frances and I enjoyed during the time we lived there. We arrived at the restaurant at 10:02 p.m., but they told us they had closed at 10:00 and sent us away, so they lost $45 ($5 x 9), plus a good tip. This branch of Kings is now out of business. There's another lesson: bend your rules a bit to serve (and keep) your customers.

Lesson 23
The Problem With Problems

Early in my business career, I was told, "If you bring me just a problem, I'll have no time for you. But bring me a problem and a possible solution, and I will have all day for you." Perhaps that position is a bit extreme, but the concept behind it is solid.

As mentors, managers, and leaders, it's our job to involve and inspire people—not to solve their problems for them. When someone comes to me with a problem and says, "What do you want me to do?," my answer is always, "Dig into the problem and come back with a recommendation on how to solve it."

Sometimes the person will solve the problem, which enables them to demonstrate their value, build their self-esteem, and earn your recognition. At the very least, it encourages the person to think about a solution—and, perhaps, to bring you an idea that gets you thinking creatively about the problem. You might not agree with what they come up with, but the person will have taken some initial steps in dealing with the issue.

Lesson 24
The Value of Consistency

One of the most important traits a leader, manager, or mentor can have is consistency. This includes treating everyone (including yourself) with respect at all times; doing what you say you'll do; and being the same person on Monday that you were last Friday.

People need consistency. It helps them know what to expect and what to do. They can't stand a boss or mentor who is a terror on Monday, Mr. Nice Guy on Tuesday and Wednesday, then a terror again. They can't adjust to the inconsistent management style.

Imagine that you drive the same route to work every day. Each day you pass a state cop who monitors your speed. You consistently drive five miles an hour over the speed limit, secure in the knowledge that this slight extra speed won't earn you a ticket. And, in fact, for two months it doesn't.

Then, one day, the cop's boss tells them, "Our budget's

been cut by five percent. We need more revenue. Give out more speeding tickets." The next day, boom! They pull you over and hand you a ticket for $112. Now you don't know what to do or what to expect next time you drive to work. You're confused, unhappy, and $112 poorer—all because of a lack of consistency. I call this lesson State Police Management.

Chapter 10
Charged With an Error

So far we had seen five games. We had taken planes, cars, trains, and a subway to get to them. We had sidestepped a hurricane on our first day, and experienced nothing but sunshine every day since then. We had met some fascinating people in airports, in restaurants, on the road, in the air, and in the hotels where we stayed. Some of these people made us feel like we were TV stars.

The boys regularly looked people in the eye, thanked them with smiles, wrote personal notes, and experienced how good that made them feel. They saw what many different people did for a living, and they also got to see that some people gave up their lives so the rest of their countrymen can live as free people.

We ate lots of great food together (in the case of us adults, way too much of it). I saw the boys become friends, sharing music and ideas, borrowing from each other, and comparing their dislikes and likes. In old baseball parks, new baseball parks, and not-built-for-baseball parks, we saw close games, blowouts, grand slams, and a manager tossed out for arguing a call.

Many people never experience all these things in a lifetime, much less in ten days. I felt grateful to live in a country where so much is possible; where people are free; where young people can not only dream, but grow up and accomplish those dreams; and where mentors can make a positive difference in the lives of those boys and girls.

Our next stop was Philadelphia. It was close enough to Pittsburgh that it made sense for us to drive there, so we rented two SUVs from Hertz. The folks at Hertz gave us platinum service at all times. In fact, initially they made a mistake with our reservation, so they apologized—and, to make amends, they let us use one of the SUVs for free. Customer service doesn't get much better than that. (We rented from Hertz throughout the trip, and we were treated well at all times. We of course sent thank-you notes to several Hertz managers—and one to the company CEO.)

To get to Philadelphia, we plugged one of Hertz's Never-Lost GPS systems into each SUV and headed east. Everyone agreed that the lady's voice giving the directions that day was much more accurate than Ellen the day before.

These road trips turned out to be great opportunities for the boys to bond. Kamerron and Sam, in particular, enjoyed being around each other. They shared lots of music, and usually swam, ate, and rode together.

On this 6½-hour trip we stopped three times—to eat, to hit the rest room, to see sights, and to meet new people. Everywhere we stopped, people smiled at us and talked with us. Usually we got to tell our story. People often replied, always with a big smile, "I wish I could go on a trip like that some day."

We reached the Embassy Suites in downtown Philadelphia about 5:30 p.m. We settled into our rooms and then took the subway to Citizens Bank Park. The Phillies were playing the Mets, and the subway was packed with fans of both teams—but mostly Mets fans. The fans—men, women, kids with their parents—were very vocal and boisterous. All had on their favorite team's hat and shirt; some had baseball gloves just in case a ball headed their way; a few looked as if they were suited up to play. Our boys heard several new and interesting words—and, for them, an unusual accent and speaking style. Fans of the opposing teams ragged on each other in a way that was friendly and insulting at the same time. But everyone obviously enjoyed it, and the fans had excitement written all over their faces.

The game was terrific, and the ballpark was out of this world. Citizens Bank Park is one of the most unusual parks in baseball. The bullpens are on two different levels, so we watched some of the pitchers warm up on the second level, well above the field. The setup reminded me of the tiered golf driving ranges in Japan.

Most of our team in front of the statue of Mike Schmidt outside Citizens Bank Park in Philadelphia.

In Philadelphia, the real contest is what goes on in the stands. The fans ragged on each other continually, arguing and shouting insults, and enjoying every minute of it. Much of the language is foul-mouthed—part of the standard ambiance of the City of Brotherly Love. But for all the arguing and name calling, we never saw anyone throw a punch. We even watched two people insult each other while they shared food from the same container. The Mets relief pitcher seemed lost coming out of the bullpen, giving up six runs in the 7th inning. The Phillies sent the Mets' fans home on the train feeling low after their 8-4 loss.

Philadelphia was one of the major cities where we spent an extra day to see the local attractions. We began with a bus tour of Philadelphia's historic sites. For the boys, the highlight of the tour was running up the steps of the Philadelphia Museum of Art—the same steps Rocky Balboa ran up many years ago, and four times since then. They ranked a visit to the Liberty Bell a close second.

Watching the Phillies and the Mets play at Citizens Bank Park in Philadelphia.

The boys gave a big thumbs-down, however, to our lunch stop, Jim's Steaks, which serves classic Philadelphia cheesesteaks. I thought the boys would be thrilled by the sandwich, which is a cross between a steak dinner and a cheeseburger—but not a single young man found it enjoyable. (My score on food recommendations involving steak was now 0-2.) Bob, who normally enjoys all kinds of food, gave Jim's a low score as well. At least Cameron made a great video of a cheesesteak being cooked.

The next morning, another important learning opportunity presented itself. As we checked out, I was told that one of the three rooms had a bill that was considerably higher than the other two. It didn't take me long to discover what had happened: one of the young men was having so much fun that he used the phone in his room to call some of his friends back home and tell them about the exciting trip. (This was back in the days before everyone over the age of five had their own cell phone. On this trip, none of the boys had his own phone.)

This was a bit of a dilemma for Gary, Bob, and me. On the one hand, because the young man had made the calls without asking us, Gary felt he should pay me for their cost. Bob didn't feel that way, though, because we hadn't explained the high cost of using hotel phones to the boys. None of them had any idea that, even though a phone call between friends costs nothing or next to nothing if it's made from the friend's home, it costs a fortune if it's made from a hotel room.

Gary, Bob, and I caucused and came up with this strategy: first we explained to the boys the financial consequences of using a hotel phone. Then we insisted that the young man who had made the calls pay a portion of the phone bill—enough for him to learn an important lesson, but not the full, exorbitant charge.

The situation reminded me of an incident from my own past. In 1952, when I was in fifth grade, my school had a PTA membership drive. The teacher wanted the class to have

100% participation. This meant that every student's parents had to either join the PTA or pay the 25¢ annual non-member fee. I knew my parents wouldn't join the PTA, but I was hoping they'd at least pay the 25¢. I asked my father for the money, and told him about the 100% participation goal, but to no avail; his answer was a polite but firm no. To this day I remember how I felt to be the only kid in the class whose parents didn't participate. I hated being the kid who kept my class from reaching its goal.

I believe that if a person takes a step toward you, you need to take two steps toward them. That's exactly what we did in the situation with the phone calls. We explained the financial ramifications of using hotel phones to everyone; the young man apologized for his mistake; he paid us a portion of the phone bill; and we all moved on. This included not dwelling on his mistake—which is why I've chosen not to identify the boy who made the error.

The same principle applies in business. I've seen supposed leaders in business and government spend way too much time trying to find someone to blame, rather than determining the cause of a problem, correcting the process, and moving forward. It's far more beneficial to learn from mistakes than to dwell on them.

Lesson 25
Get the Facts Before Making a Decision

Getting the facts before making a decision is important for three reasons. First, it puts you in a better position to make a wise decision. Second, the process gives you more time to make the right decision. And third, you will be seen as consistent, reliable, logical, and trustworthy.

Yet too many leaders *don't* always get the facts before they make decisions. If you want a good example, ask your Congressman if they read the whole 2000-page health-care reform bill before voting on it.

My grandmother used to tell me that there are always three sides to every story: what Person A said, what Person B said, and what really happened. Before you make a decision, listen to each person's side, get as much information as possible, and sort out the facts from the opinions as best you can.

A situation I faced a few years ago helped cement this lesson for me. One of our minority employees had filed a complaint with our HR Department. She insisted that she had been unfairly passed over for a position for which she claimed she was highly qualified.

My first step was to meet with her supervisor and her team of coworkers. Their side of the story was that, although the employee was good at what she did, she wasn't dependable.

I then talked to the young woman. She explained that she had in fact missed some days of work because she was pregnant and going to college at night. She also said that she had filed a complaint because, at a previous employer, she had needed to do so in order to be treated fairly. I asked her to tell me that story. She told me that, at her previous employer, she had tested for a position and exceeded the requirements, but the job was given to a friend of her supervisor. When she asked why she had been passed over, she was told that she didn't have the required experience. She filed a complaint, won, and got the job for which she was qualified. She told me that she wanted to make sure that something similar wasn't happening now.

As I looked into the situation, it became clear that no one was lying or trying to mislead me. But I was able to verify that what the young woman said contained the most truth. I had our company give her the job, and she has done well at it ever since. We also began paying her college tuition, and she received her degree two years later.

Over the years, I've learned several useful principles that apply to this process:

- Don't assume anything, especially about who's right and who's wrong. Instead, ask questions of all the relevant stakeholders.

- Don't rush to make a decision too quickly. If there's no genuine need to hurry, don't.

- When making (or reversing) a decision, ask yourself and others why: *Why is this the best (or the right) deci-*

sion? Why should we do things this way? Why should we not do any of the reasonable alternatives?

- Also ask: *What issues or difficulties might this decision generate? What might each of the reasonable alternatives generate?*

- Throughout the process, keep your emotions under control. If you're tempted to make a decision based just on your emotions, stop and take a walk around the block. This is just as important for positive emotions, such as excitement and anticipation, as it is for negative ones.

- When you write a letter or e-mail announcing a big decision, put yourself in your readers' shoes. Imagine how they will react. When the letter or e-mail is done, don't send it immediately. Let it sit overnight first.

If we don't get the facts before making a decision—whether it involves a young person we're mentoring or a business we're running—the consequences could be dire.

Lesson 26
GPS and Life

For a GPS system to work properly, you first need to program in your destination. After that, you have some choices:

the fastest route, the slower but safer route, the scenic route, etc. In all cases, though, you're much less likely to get lost if you know exactly where you want to end up.

Success follows this same principle. The clearer you are about where you want to go, the less likely you are to get lost, and the more likely you are to get there.

An effective mentor can not only help a mentee decide on their destination, but can serve as their GPS, guiding them to make wise choices along the way, and warning them of the consequences of unwise ones.

Lesson 27
Shout Compliments; Whisper Criticism

Sadly, a high percentage of today's leaders say little when people succeed, but make lots of noise when those folks fall short or make a mistake. They need to do just the opposite.

Some of these leaders eventually realize that a public dressing down is neither good for the employee nor good for business. But then they may apologize in the quietness of their office, with only the employee in attendance. Worse, they may wait until weeks or months later, at the employee's performance review. Worse still, they may over-apologize, embarrassing both themselves and the employee.

Few people relish criticism. Even fewer welcome it in front of other people. Yet I have learned that almost everyone will accept legitimate criticism if it is properly delivered—privately and one to one, with an emphasis on helping the person improve their performance. You need to be clear that you are criticizing their action, not them personally. You also need to be very specific about what the problem is and what they might do differently next time, so they can learn from their error.

In my 40+ years in business, the criticism that had the most profound and positive effect on me was when my boss called me into his office and said, in a normal business tone, "I was surprised to see you handle that issue that way. Tell me why you did it that way." I got the message immediately—and the lesson stuck with me.

There is an art to giving compliments, too.

First, be on the lookout for the things that people do right—and compliment them for doing them right.

Second, the compliment must be sincere. People can spot a phony a mile away. In fact, a phony compliment is twice as bad as no compliment at all.

A compliment also needs to be very specific. You need to say exactly *what* the person did well and why what they did was valuable or important.

Lastly, tone and appearance can be as important as content. When you give a compliment, do it with passion in your voice and eyes. If possible, do it in front of a lot of the person's peers. If it's an e-mail compliment, send it in large colored letters. My employees at Touchstone value these "shout-outs" a great deal.

This lesson works just as well with children, students, and mentees as it does with employees.

Chapter 11
The World Champion of Cities

After two days in Philly, we turned in our SUVs and boarded a train for New York City. I was sure this two-hour ride would be one of the highlights of the trip for the boys, but I was wrong again. Most of them slept almost the entire way.

The boys did fall in love with the Big Apple, though. They were awestruck by the buildings, the lights, the people, and the energized atmosphere.

The ambience of New York has changed dramatically since I lived there in 1964. Back then, people were often rude and callous. But our group was helped by total strangers everywhere we went. Once, as we stood on a street corner, uncertain where to find our subway stop, a man coming out of a nearby coffee shop read the dilemma on our faces. We must have looked as lost as last year's Easter egg. He stopped, asked us where we wanted to go, and walked us to the right subway entrance.

A few hours later, a garbage collector stopped what he was doing and asked us where we were from. When we told him about our trip, he took off his gloves, shook everyone's hands, and said, "I wish I could go along with you all to the game tonight." By now, of course, that phrase had become our background chorus.

One of the things the boys wanted to see was Ground Zero, the site of the destroyed World Trade Center. It was less than a half-hour walk from the Embassy Suites, so we visited this first.

Seeing the bare metal beams where buildings used to be brought back strong memories for me. On the morning of September 11, 2001, I was on an American Airlines flight headed to Reagan Airport in Washington when the first plane hit the World Trade Center. Fortunately, we were only 30 minutes out of Dallas when the nation's airspace was closed, so we simply returned to the Dallas airport. All the information we passengers had at the time was from a person in front of me who had read on his phone that a plane had hit one of the towers.

The boys stared at the site, silent and reverent. There was little talking and no grabbing and pushing. Sam put it best when he wrote in his journal:

> *It was sad seeing the site. It was weird that when they found the beams that were left that they made a cross.*

Bob said, "It's unbelievable that airplanes could have knocked these buildings down."

That night's ball game was between the Yankees and the Mets in Yankee Stadium. To our surprise, Cameron was refused entrance because video cameras were not allowed in the stadium. Since we were a long way from the hotel, we had to figure out what to do with the camera. We asked a nearby policeman for advice, and he told us there was a business across the street where you could check video cameras and other prohibited items. Someone had taken the coat check business to a new level. We checked the video camera, went into Yankee Stadium, and found our seats deep in center field, in the bench seats section.

It didn't take us long to realize that the verbal battles we had recently witnessed between Phillies and Mets fans were Pee-Wee League competitions compared to the face-offs between Mets and Yankees supporters. We were seated among some Yankees fans and many Mets fans, and the two groups went at it from the moment the game began. I didn't know whether to laugh, cringe, or ignore the invective and just watch the game. I wound up doing a little of each. (No matter how much verbal fur flew, however, no one actually shoved or hit anybody, just like in Philadelphia.)

It was a good game and a classic face-off: Mets vs. Yankees, Pedro Martinez vs. Mike Mussina. The Yankees got on the scoreboard first, when Derek Jeter met Pedro with a lead-off homer. The Yankees fans went crazy. But the Mets struck back and took a commanding lead after a few innings. The Yankees had already lost two in a row, and when the team fell behind, the Yankees fans turned on their own players. This was not fun to watch or listen to. I wouldn't want to get on these fans' bad sides. The Mets won the game, 6-4.

We also got some bonus entertainment from the Yankees' grounds crew between the sixth and seventh innings. These skilled employees taught us a lesson: don't be afraid to do things differently.

Just like at other stadiums, the Yankees' grounds crew grooms the infield after the sixth inning. But at Yankee Stadium, the song "YMCA" is played while they do it—and the grounds crew puts down their rakes and performs the YMCA dance moves. This was way more fun than in Cincinnati, where someone simply drove around the infield on a little cub tractor. The grounds crew in New York reminded us that there is usually more than one way to do things well—and sometimes you can do things well and have fun at the same time.

Yankee Stadium itself was disappointing. It was loaded with history, but it was obvious that George Steinbrenner was more interested in securing a new stadium than in keeping up this one.

We spent the next day touring the city. We began with a ride on a double-decker tour bus, which was another first for most of the boys. We saw Times Square, Harlem, the theater district, and many other sites. Some of the young men fell asleep, but Matt was mesmerized by the tall buildings, the lights, and the people everywhere. He so enjoyed the city that he told his mom that New York was where he wanted to live. Here is what he wrote in his journal:

Today we arrived in New York City, and it is every-thing I expected. It's big, populated, and exciting. There are a lot of things to do, so I doubt we will get bored. My favorite place was Times Square. I was blown away by the huge billboards and advertise-ments.

One of the highlights of our stay in New York was our visit to Wall Street. Cameron had asked me many questions about stocks during our trip; now he and the other young men had an opportunity to see the stock market close up. I wouldn't be surprised if at least one of the boys becomes a banker some day. At the Stock Exchange Building, we explained how and where companies raise money and how stock is sold. We also discussed how, over the long term, the stock market has routinely outperformed most other invest-ments.

As we left the Stock Exchange Building, I looked at the expressions on the boys' faces and thought, *What a difference this day has made for these boys. But it's not rocket science. Gary, Bob, and I aren't teaching the boys Latin. All we're do-ing is having fun with them and seeing some sights together. Everyone can do this.*

People often say they don't have time to get involved with other people's kids. I challenge that excuse. The ques-tion everyone has to answer is, *How can I not find two hours a week to help a child?*—because often two or three hours a week is all it takes to turn a child's life around.

This is doubly true if a child has one or more parents in prison. Without some better role model—or some type of intervention—71% of those kids will end up in prison themselves.

As I pondered this, Sam looked at me and said what all of us were feeling: "You know what? I can't wait until tomorrow." Andy said, "Today was pretty cool." Spencer wrote in his journal:

> *We went back to the room and went straight to bed because we were so tired.*

Lesson 28
Expect, Demonstrate, and Then Follow Up

I often hear people say that the greatest athletes and leaders are born with exceptional talent. I disagree. While it's true that some positive traits are passed on through the gene pool, that's not what leads to great success.

Most of the exceptional people I know, or have seen in action, do three things: they make their expectations very clear; they demonstrate what they consider successful or desirable performance; and they follow up—multiple times, if necessary—until they catch people doing it right, and then they acknowledge the accomplishment.

Follow-up turns out to be the key. If you set one clear expectation, demonstrate exactly what you want, and follow up properly and repeatedly, you'll create one excellent result. If you have a laundry list of expectations and demonstrate clearly what you want for each, but don't carefully follow up multiple times, you'll wind up with many poor results, many unfulfilled expectations, and possibly an ulcer. The choice is yours.

Expectation

With employees, kids, and even ourselves, it's crucial for us to know *exactly* what we expect, and to communicate those expectations equally clearly, in sufficient detail. "I expect you to be prompt" raises more questions than it answers. Is it okay to be two minutes late? Five? Ten? But in the statement that follows, there's no uncertainty about the speaker's expectations. "We start at 8:00—not 8:01 and not 7:59. That's when I expect you to be here, ready to roll. That means getting here well before 8:00, so that you're ready by 8:00."

It's just as critical to express our expectations in a positive way. The speaker in the above paragraph is firm but positive. Compare their words with these: "I don't tolerate latecomers. If you're not ready by 8:00, I'll ding you for it." Which approach is more supportive and empowering?

100% of leaders, mentors, and parents have little trouble communicating their expectations. It's the other two parts of the sequence, demonstration and follow-up, where they're more likely to fall short.

Demonstration

Demonstration is the art of showing people exactly what to do, how to do it, and when to do it. Most of us don't clearly and consistently demonstrate what we expect. This is partly because we don't believe we need to. We assume that if we explain our expectations clearly, then the actions required to fulfill them will be obvious.

This simply isn't so. People learn by observing, doing, and practicing—not just by being told. And part of being a good manager, leader, mentor, or parent is showing others exactly what creates the best results.

So don't just tell or explain. Demonstrate clearly, in detail, precisely what you want or expect—multiple times, if necessary.

Demonstrating what you want also includes consistently modeling what you expect from others. If you ask your employees to trust you, you need to show trust in them. But if your car is full of clutter, your kids aren't going to take you seriously when you lecture them on cleaning their rooms. And if you're not good about returning phone calls, your employees aren't going to believe you when you talk about the virtues of responsive customer service. If you say X but do Y, expect the people you lead or mentor to become proficient at Y.

Demonstration isn't only about what you do, however; it's also about what you *don't* do. If you avoid or refuse to deal with certain situations, you're modeling and teaching avoidance. Is that what you want others to learn from you?

Lastly, an essential piece of demonstration is consistency. When your beliefs, values, and actions are all consistent—and when you consistently demonstrate the same things in the same way—then what you model sinks in deeply. In contrast, if you're inconsistent in any substantive way, you end up not demonstrating anything—or, worse, you demonstrate that you're capricious and unreliable. People then learn to organize their own behavior around your mood.

The men, women, girls, and boys who look up to you will copy what you do. It's up to you to make sure that what you do is worth copying.

Follow-Up

This is where most of us drop the ball. We expect people to do exactly what we want them to do—and to consistently do it well—just because we showed them or told them how. In fact, this rarely happens. Learning requires practice, and often supervision.

We all know this from the ball field. No decent Little League coach would hit a pitch over the fence, tell the kids, "That's how you hit a home run," and then expect them to routinely knock pitches out of the park. Yet, metaphorically, this is what many of us do with our employees and mentees.

When I played baseball growing up, every coach watched me, encouraged me, corrected me, and acknowledged my accomplishments. They provided consistent, immediate follow-up until I was able to correctly do what they asked of me, day after day, on my own.

Nothing is more important than follow-up. Keep observing, encouraging, and correcting people until they get it right. And when you catch them doing it right, acknowledge them for it immediately. This ensures that they will want to do it right again. Nothing feels better than being caught succeeding, and being appreciated for it. And the more things someone does right, the more they can and will accomplish.

So don't just tell people to do things. Only initiate things you're actually going to thoroughly follow up on, multiple times. People *will* do the things you follow up on. Your follow-up tells them that those things are important to you. They also know their own butts are on the line.

If you don't follow up, or follow up half-heartedly, people may or may not do what you expect, because you've sent them this message: *This particular task isn't really that important to me.* Employees figure this out quickly; kids figure it out even faster.

In expecting, demonstrating, and following up, most people reverse the emphasis that's needed for success. They expect too much, demonstrate too little, and follow up *way* too little.

Instead, try this: start with high but realistic expectations. Get totally clear about those expectations, and then make them equally clear to everyone involved. Next, demonstrate exactly what you expect, in detail, multiple times (and, if necessary, on a regular basis). Then follow up, over and over and over, with encouragement, correction, and (when people do it right) acknowledgement.

The result will be people who do the right thing well, and who are *proud* to do the right thing well, time after time.

Lesson 29
Outwork Your Competition (and Your Peers)

Early in my career, I was able to get ahead of everyone else because I worked longer hours. I also worked harder, staying focused on each task. As a result, I was promoted first to manager, then group manager, then regional manager, and eventually to president of the 42nd largest company in the U.S. There was no secret to my success. I simply worked longer and harder than my peers (and the people above me, too).

Some years ago, a newly promoted senior VP came to me to thank me for my help and support. But then he asked me what he needed to do to become an executive VP. I got up, shut my office door, and gave him the following answer: "For every new position and every new role I've accepted, I approached it as if it would be the last job of my career. I did it as if someone else was after it, and as if I meant to keep it forever. This meant working hard and working smart—focusing on the job at hand, meeting my plan, and thinking and executing for the long term. I also tried to create an organization where the results would continue to improve after I left or retired." I added, "I also felt that if I didn't approach my job in this way, then someone else would—and should—take my place."

For some years I've run Touchstone, a large call center in Pakistan. It's been successful in many ways, but not because

I'm a genius at leading. I've simply given the business a lot of my time and personal attention. I go to Pakistan every six months to help with hiring and training, to get to know my employees better, and to inspire them one on one. They see how hard I work, and the work ethic naturally transfers to them.

Before I opened my company in Pakistan, I talked by phone with someone who used to work for me. He ran a call center, though his was based in India. I asked him how his business was doing, and he said, "Terrible. The guy I've hired to run it doesn't hire good people. He runs his own call center, too, and he hires all the good people for his own operations and hires the dregs for mine." I asked him, "When was the last time you were in India?" He said, "I've never been there, and I'm not going." Is it any wonder his business didn't do well? You can't run any business in your spare time or from 11,000 miles away.

It's not that this fellow, or the people working for him, are lazy. But they were satisfied with the status quo. Those of us who are willing to work harder are going to out-compete him every time.

Outworking your competition is just as important in nonprofit ventures. Over the past 15 years, I and a small group of friends have raised over $10 million for three nonprofits. How? We began with an intelligent plan and worked hard—lots of hours, lots of attention, lots of focus, week after week. It's a simple strategy, and it works. We have been successful year after year because we all kept a simple commitment to hard work.

Chapter 12
Good Manners, Clean Clothes, and Discipline

We headed out of New York City in two SUVs from Hertz, their GPS systems programmed to direct us to Worcester, Massachusetts, about 45 miles west of Boston. Rocco Leone, an ex-colleague of mine, had invited us to stop on our way to Bean Town to have dinner with him, his wife Donna, and his five beautiful daughters. When an Italian invites you to join his family for dinner, you'd be a fool to say no. But Rocco and his wife Donna were also smart enough not to try to make dinner for eleven guests, eight of whom had bottomless pits for stomachs. Instead, they asked us to join them at a first-rate Italian restaurant.

Up to this point, the only times I had seen all the boys quiet at once was when they were eating or sleeping. That evening we discovered a third way to settle them down: put them around a table with pretty girls. All the boys were on their best behavior—no pinching each other (or the girls), no burping, no other body noises.

Until today, we had spent each night in Embassy Suites hotels, where each suite had a bedroom with two beds and a living room with a convertible sofa. This arrangement comfortably accommodated three people, and, with a rolling cot added, not-so-comfortably accommodated four. But Worcester had no Embassy Suites, so we had reserved rooms in a Marriott Courtyard, which was much less luxurious.

Before this trip, most of the boys had never flown in a plane, stayed in a hotel, or eaten in restaurants for more than two meals in a row. By now, though, they had become seasoned travelers and experienced hotel and food critics. Sam wrote in his journal, *The room was really small.* Cameron had more of a reason to gripe: *We stayed at the Marriott. It had no couch, and Kamerron and I had to share a bed.* Some of the boys also complained that the pool was too small and not very deep.

Tonight was laundry night. Gary, Bob, and I were not surprised to discover that none of the eight boys had ever washed their own clothes before. We gave them instructions on how to use the nearby laundromat's washers and dryers. They quickly discovered that doing laundry wasn't that difficult—though a few used too much soap. Everyone left with clean, fresh-smelling clothes, although the laundromat looked somewhat worse for wear. Doing their own laundry was a good learning experience for the young men, though, and something they should be required to do more often.

Many times during our trip, I marveled at how much more knowledgeable, worldly, and inquisitive these boys were than I was at their age. All of them were kind, personable, and respectful to others (though not always to each other). But every one of them—some more than others—lacked self-discipline. I saw it in the way they handled money, how they packed, how they followed instructions, and their personal hygiene.

We Americans need to do more with discipline in raising our kids—and, in many cases, in living our own lives. The key is teaching and demonstrating self-discipline from the time our kids are very small. We can expend a little time and energy now, or a lot more later. (You may remember the old Fram oil filter commercial, which made the same point. You could pay a little more for a Fram oil filter now, or pay a lot more in repairs later.)

Many people today misinterpret the word *discipline* to mean punishment. But the word has many other, more positive attributes. When I was young, my father taught me that in order to get something I wanted in the future, I had to have the discipline to be prudent, to save, and to wait.

He also taught me to have the discipline to get the facts before making a decision. I'll give my age away here, but when I was 14, I saved enough money to buy a pair of white buck shoes for school. I remember how they looked – white with a reddish sole. Boy, I felt like a million bucks, but it took only a few weeks until the newness rubbed off. The shoes got dirty, and I ended up dying them black. My dad was very gracious. He bought the dye and didn't rub it in (on me, I mean). All I could think about was the money I wasted.

Those lessons served me well growing up, and they continue to serve me well today.

My ex-boss (and former Chairman and Chief Executive Officer of Associates), Reece Overcash, often said that the keys to success were the three I's: integrity, intelligence, and intensity. I agreed that these were essential, but I also told Reece that for these three words to be meaningful, you have to add discipline. Without discipline, it's easy to burn out, lose focus or faith, or simply give up.

I smoked three packs a day when I was in my 20s. I stopped on New Year's Day of 1968. Discipline got me through those first few smoke-free days. So did food. In fact, like many ex-smokers, I gained 35 pounds over the next few months. But when someone told me I looked like the Pillsbury Doughboy, I started doing sit-ups. I did 600 a night for six years, missing a total of one night. Discipline was the key to maintaining this practice. Most of the time I didn't want to do the sit-ups, but I did them anyway. As a result, I lost the weight—and, in the decades since then, continued discipline has enabled me to keep it off.

With one exception, of course. During this trip with eight human garbage disposals, I put on 20 pounds. It took three months of extra self-discipline to shed them afterward.

Even though the boys complained about our hotel, everyone slept well that night. We woke up refreshed, excited, and ready to make our way to Boston.

Lesson 30
Intelligence, Intensity, and Integrity—
Plus Discipline

My former boss, Reece Overcash, mentored many young people and set the standard for community volunteering at Associates. Reece always rated people on three scales—the 3 I's:

Intelligence: Is the person logical? Do they use common sense? Do they learn from the mistakes they make?

Intensity: Do they make their job, their family, and God their highest priorities?

Integrity: Is the person honest with themselves? (Reece believed—correctly, in my view—that if you couldn't be honest with yourself, no one could trust you over the long term.)

Without sufficient self-discipline, you would be intelligent only some of the time; you would ease up on the intensity some of the time; and you would slack off on integrity once in a while, especially during stressful times. But self-discipline enables you to *always* live according to the 3 I's, no matter what your circumstances.

Chapter 13
Two Oldies But Goodies

In Boston, we were back at the Embassy Suites, with three two-room suites and a large pool. The boys were also back to their old noisy selves.

We spent the day touring. We visited the harbor where the Boston Tea Party took place; a street where Paul Revere rode, yelling, "The British are coming!"; and many more historical sites. But the boys were not impressed as much as they were in Philadelphia and New York. In fact, as one young man wrote in his journal, *Boston is a nice city, but it bored me.*

In the afternoon we visited Massachusetts Institute of Technology, where Gary Randle's daughter was attending summer school. We were the guests of Carl Reid, MIT's Director of Undergraduate Admissions. Mr. Reid took the boys on a short tour and gave each one an MIT t-shirt afterward.

I'd wanted all the boys to tour the campus of one of the most selective colleges in the country. I also wanted them to imagine themselves someday attending MIT, or an equally good school. Since the boys ranged in age from 12 through 16, I worried a bit that MIT wouldn't interest them, but once again they proved me wrong. The visit made a big impression on them, and four of the six boys wrote about their tour in their journals. In Cameron's journal, the tour and the t-shirts got as much attention and praise as the dinner with Rocco and his daughters the previous night. Andy was also impressed with the gift of the MIT t-shirt.

That evening we took the subway to Fenway Park, where the Red Sox faced off against the Mets. It was a perfect baseball evening: warm, no clouds, a sold-out stadium, and seats behind home plate. Spencer chose to wear his Yankees hat, which earned him lots of dirty looks from Red Sox fans (and some real headaches the next day).

All of us were eager to experience Fenway, which is the oldest of all the Major League parks, and one of only three built before 1960. It's got an unusual layout, with a very shallow left field that ends in the Green Monster, the famous 37-foot-tall fence. Everything was in immaculate condition, even though the park was built in 1912. The Red Sox fans were different from the fans in New York and Philly: they focused on the game instead of trying to out-shout the people next to them, but they were in on every pitch.

The Fenway groundskeepers impressed me, too. They were very focused and professional, even perfectionist, making sure that every part of the infield met their standards.

They reminded me of the janitor at NASA who, when asked what he did for a living, replied, "I help put men on the moon."

I also thought that not selling beer in the stands was a nice family touch—and probably a wise safety measure, too. When you have to get up from your seat to get your own beer, you're more likely to realize when you've had enough alcohol.

All of us enjoyed the game, the food, and the Fenway atmosphere. The Red Sox won their seventh game in a row; a home run by Manny Ramirez led the way to a 12-8 victory.

Afterward we took the subway back to the Embassy Suites. We mistakenly got off a stop too soon—we could have used a NeverLost GPS, like the ones in our SUVs—but Bob used his internal compass to point us in the right direction, and we were back at the hotel in half an hour.

The next morning we got up and checked out very early, in order to catch a 7:30 plane to Chicago. We had no trouble until we reached Logan Airport, where Spencer found out the hard way that if you give it out, you better learn to take it.

Spencer wore his Yankees hat into the airport. This is perfectly legal, of course, but it's not the smartest thing to do in a city that's had a century-long rivalry with the Yankees. The TSA people took one look at Spencer's hat and, very politely, pulled him aside and gave him a full screening. This amused all the other boys, but they learned an important lesson: the higher a monkey climbs up a pole, the more people can see him scratch his butt. The incident also helped the boys better understand why I make a point of arriving early.

The flight was smooth and uneventful. We landed in Chicago, picked up our two SUVs (with GPS systems, of course), and arrived at the Embassy Suites about lunchtime. We had the afternoon to rest, and then went for dinner at the world-famous Gino's, which serves some of the best deep-dish Chicago-style pizza. I was curious to see if any of the boys would order steak or a hamburger. They didn't; it was pizza all around. It was a wise choice, too; we all agreed that Gino's pizza earned its world-famous designation.

Sam, Kamerron, Cameron, Andy, Spencer, and Matt just after dinner at Gino's East in Chicago.

We spent the evening touring Chicago on O'Leary's Fire Truck, which took us to the spots where many of Chicago's big fires had begun, including the one in 1871 that burned most of the city. We also saw the Chicago skyline, the Lake Michigan shoreline, and Soldier Field (a highlight of

Cameron's day), where the Bears play football. We ended the day with dessert at Cold Stone Creamery.

The next afternoon we took the L—Chicago's system of elevated trains—to the Cubs game at Wrigley Field. It was another beautiful day—sunshine and 75 degrees.

Wrigley Field is the second-oldest park in Major League Baseball, built in 1914, only two years after Fenway Park. Wrigley Field has been called "what every baseball park wants to be." It is a wonderful ballpark, with ivy-covered walls, and people sitting on the roof in both right and left fields. We had great seats, just to the right of home plate.

In front of the Harry Caray statue outside Wrigley Field in Chicago.

The game itself—the Cubs vs. the Milwaukee Brewers—was something of a disappointment. There was no spectacular fielding play, no grand slam, no string of hits, no come-from-behind rally. Both teams played competent but unmemorable baseball. The Cubs won the game 2-0.

Still, we all had a good time. The people who worked at Wrigley Field were very friendly and helpful, the stadium was grand, and the weather was perfect. None of us really cared who won and who lost. At this point in our travels, we had become hardcore fans of the game, not of any team.

We had our picture taken by the Harry Caray statue outside the stadium, then took the L back to our hotel. We packed up, loaded our gear into our SUVs, and began the 90-minute drive to our final stop, Milwaukee.

Lesson 31
Read, Read, Read

I encourage everyone to read all kinds of books: history, business, mysteries, biographies of sports heroes. Read the newspaper, sports magazines, and business journals. Read in front of your children, so they will pick up the habit. Require your subordinates to read books that can help them at work.

Better yet, recommend specific books, and give them copies. Every employee in our company has read Jim

Collins's *Good to Great*, and I've also given many people Jack Mitchell's *Hug Your Customers*.

There is no better gift than a book—except the gift of teaching someone to read.

Lesson 32
As You Climb the Ladder

The higher you climb up the ladder of success, the more attention you draw from people. Not all of this is good attention. There will be folks who will want to learn from you, and friends and allies who will be pleased to see you succeed—but there will also be others who will be envious of your position, and who will want you to fail.

All of these groups will be watching you carefully. So conduct yourself honorably and professionally at all times—in what you do, what you say, and what you write.

Bob Hunter, one of the best executives I know, had a powerful technique that he used with each young hotshot that got promoted. He called the person into his office and went through the normal speech we all give to newly promoted up-and-comers. But Bob ended each such meeting by saying, "Several people here were disappointed that they didn't get the promotion you did, but there's only one person who has the power to scuttle it. Do you want to know who that is?" "Yes," the newly promoted man or woman always said. Bob smiled and said, "All right. Here's their picture." And he handed the person a mirror.

When everyone is watching you carefully, you need to watch yourself even more carefully. *You* are responsible for the actions you take and the choices you make, and these will become the true measure of your success over time.

Chapter 14
Rounding Third and Heading Home

Somehow, even with a NeverLost GPS system in each SUV, Bob and I got separated as we headed to Milwaukee. But we were seasoned travelers, so there was no panic or confusion. We took different routes but arrived at our hotel within minutes of each other.

The drive to Milwaukee without food had made our entire team hungry. We went to dinner at a Texas Roadhouse, where we ate our usual meal of choice: steaks (big ones), baked potatoes, and French fries. (After the trip, when I went back and reread the boys' journals, Texas Roadhouse was the only restaurant mentioned—and praised—in all of them.)

The following day we planned to take a tour of the Harley-Davidson factory. Some of the boys hadn't brought long pants, which are required for the tour, so our next stop was

Target. The boys were efficient shoppers: they found the right size pants, bought them, and left. This took all of ten minutes.

The next morning we headed out for Harley-Davidson. My friend Clyde Fessler, who was instrumental in developing Harley-Davidson into the powerhouse it is today, had arranged the tour for us. The boys enjoyed the beginning of the tour—especially seeing all the shiny new Harleys—but their interest waned surprisingly quickly. They were turned off by the assembly lines and the industrial machinery. I remember thinking, *I think we have more future bankers than factory workers in this bunch.*

When we got back to the hotel, we sat down as a group for our second formal meeting since the trip began. We reviewed what the group had done over the past 20 days. We learned to recognize good service and to thank people in writing. We learned to plan together, respect each other (most of the time), wash clothes, schedule our time, and follow that schedule. (This included using public bathrooms without holding up the whole group.) We learned about our country, many of our cities, and some of the people who live in those cities. We also learned about each other—and about ourselves. And we learned many of the ways in which baseball mimics life.

I made sure that all the boys had completed their journals, then collected those journals and their cameras.

Our final agenda item was voting for the winners of several awards. Only the boys could vote for these, and only the boys could receive them. The winners were:

- Neatest: This award was partly for the traveler who kept his belongings, and his part of his hotel room, the most orderly. But it was intended even more for the boy who had the best traveling demeanor. Matt was the shining example on both counts, and the winner of this award.

- Messiest: Spencer was the winner, by a landslide. If Matt was a 10 on the neatness scale, Spencer was a 1. Reports of his messiness came from every adult who shared a room with him. The clincher was Spencer's gym bag, which—as a result of his cramming clothes into it—had been held together by duct tape since we left Boston.

- Most talkative: The winner was Sam, whom we eventually began calling Grasshopper. Sam rarely missed an opportunity to meet and greet.

- Quietest: The winner was the fellow we often called Big Quiet: Matt. The nickname says it all.

Each of the winners received an extra dessert that evening.

There was no award for most respectful, but here's what Bob Meyer (remember, we adults had to keep journals, too) wrote in his journal:

I would have picked Cameron as most respectful.... He is quick with "please," "thank you," "yes, sir," and "no, sir." He responds well to authority. He is very patient with me and my hearing problem. He doesn't mind repeating things multiple times and slowing down so I can understand.

After dinner that evening, we headed to Miller Park, where we took a group picture in front of the bronze statue of Hank Aaron. Aaron was a Big Brother in Atlanta, an outstanding mentor, and an eloquent speaker, especially on the topic of mentoring. I had the good fortune to meet in him in 1999, when he and I were involved in a BBBS gala in Fort Worth, so that photo has special meaning for me.

Sam, Kamerron, Spencer, Cameron, Andy, and Matt in front of the commemorative statue of Hank Aaron outside Milwaukee's Miller Park.

At the BBBS gala there was a silent auction and a live auction. There were many items with a Texas flair in the silent auction, one of which was luggage that was designed for only a Texan. Aaron had his eye on the luggage and placed a bid on it. I then noticed that our head of corporate communications was actually bidding against Aaron. After three increases in the bid I told Sandy, "Please let Aaron buy the luggage; if you want, I'll get you another set." Aaron got the luggage and made a great speech in front of the 800 people in attendance. I kept the bid sheet with Aaron's signatures.

Miller Park, like the new stadiums we visited in Atlanta, Cincinnati, Pittsburgh, and Philadelphia, was beautiful. It was built in 2001 and has a retractable roof that can close in just ten minutes. The weather was very cool and damp this first of July, so the game was played under the dome.

The employees at Miller Park were very friendly. One of the ladies at the concession stand explained the difference between a hot dog and a brat. Now I know: the difference is in the taste.

The game between the Brewers and Pittsburgh was close and very exciting, and included three home runs. The Brewers won by a score of 8-4.

We returned to our hotel tired and happy. But we were also a bit sad, because tomorrow morning our trip would end. For three weeks, our motley crew had lived together, eaten together, traveled together, and enjoyed baseball together. A day from now we'd all be back home with stories to tell, pictures to share, and, for us adults, extra pounds to lose.

Here's how three of our young men summarized the trip. Kamerron wrote in his journal:

The whole trip to me was fun. We had good seats the whole trip, especially in Atlanta. Box seats and free food. We stayed in hotels, and we went to so many restaurants. I can't remember them all.

Cameron made this observation in his journal:

I liked the trip very much. My love of baseball increased. I also made friends as we travelled from ballpark to ballpark.

It was my grandson Sam who offered the pithiest comment, however. On this last evening together, he said to me, "I'm going to miss my friends—and getting paid every day. I hope we can do it again some time."

Lesson 33
Surround Yourself with Good People

"Good people" means people you can trust and depend on, and who have the same values as you.

"Good people" also means folks who are strong in areas where you are not.

I urge every employee—and every leader—to do a thorough and honest self-assessment. Make two lists, side by side: one of your strengths, the other of your weaknesses.

If you're a leader or manager, hire someone who is strong in those areas where you are weak. Then you'll both be working with good people—and you'll be able to cover each other's back.

Extra Inning

In 2010, a miracle happened: the Rangers made it not only to the playoffs, but to the World Series. They got murdered by the Giants in only five games—but I'm optimistic about their chances in the future. With hard work, discipline, and some of the lessons in this book (I plan to give copies to the Rangers' owners), maybe they'll become world champions once again.

Acknowledgments

My profound thanks to the parents and guardians of the young men who were part of this journey. Without the approval and encouragement of these caring, trusting adults, the trip would never have taken place.

My thanks to all the gracious folks at Embassy Suites, who consistently treated us like minor royalty, and to the equally warm and helpful people at Hertz, who always went the extra mile for us. Other large organizations can learn a great deal from the way these two fine companies serve their customers.

As always, I reserve my deepest gratitude of all for my wife Frances.

About the Author

Tom Slone is Chairman and CEO of Touchstone Communications in Southlake, Texas. He and three other executives founded Touchstone in 2002 to provide offshore business process outsourcing (BPO) solutions to the financial services industry in the U.S. and U.K.

Before founding Touchstone Communications, Tom was president of consumer operations (the largest consumer operation in the world) at Associates First Capital, which included Transouth, First Family, Kentucky Finance, AHES, and consumer branches in the U.S., the U.K., Puerto Rico, Ireland, and Canada. At the time of his retirement from Associates, he was responsible for assets of $33 billion and

14,000 employees. In 2000 he was awarded the American Financial Services Association Distinguished Service Award.

Tom holds a bachelor's degree in psychology from the University of Pittsburgh, where he is a Director of the Alumni Board and a member of the Board of Visitors. He also established the university's Tom R. Slone Scholarship. In 2005, Tom received the university's Legacy Laureate Award. In addition, Tom served on the Executive Advisory Board of the Department of Marketing and Logistics at the University of North Texas.

Tom is a long-time volunteer with Big Brothers Big Sisters of America, and the past chairman of the Tarrant County, Texas BBBS agency. He recently led a fund drive that generated $1 million for a new gym at H.O.P.E. Farm (located in Fort Worth). He also led a drive to create a Pakistan Chair at the University of Texas, raising over half a million dollars for the program.

Tom and his wife Frances live in Colleyville, Texas. They have four children and seven grandchildren.